D0526435

B1

THE REIVERS WAY

Allendale from near Staward Pele

THE REIVERS WAY

by

JAMES ROBERTS

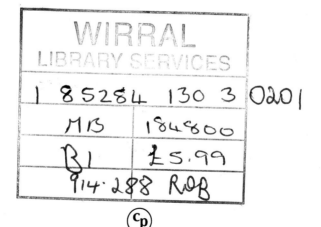

CICERONE PRESS
MILNTHORPE, CUMBRIA

In Memoriam
Jonathan Moyle (1961-1990)

Do not go gentle into that good night
Rage, rage against the dying of the light

Dylan Thomas

Acknowledgements

My thanks are due to the John Steele at the Northumberland National Park office in Rothbury, for his assistance and advice; to Brian and Valerie Smart in Wooler for their marvellous hospitality, to Aidan Robertson, Emma and Oliver Fryer, John and Katy Wood, and especially to Kev Reynolds for his wonderful help and support. Most of all I owe thanks to my wife Elena, who found her honeymoon turned into a research expedition and who supported me through many sleepless nights over a word processor. This book is dedicated to Elena.

Front Cover: Bamburgh Castle from the Stag Rocks
(Photo: B.Evans)

CONTENTS

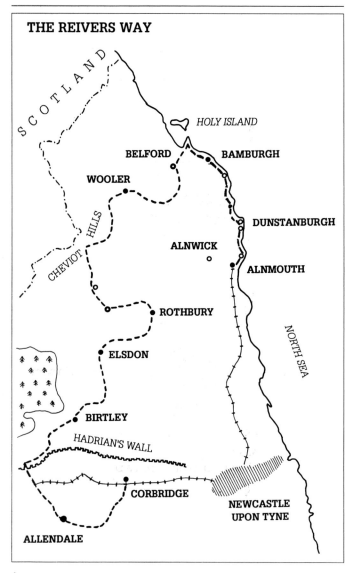

INTRODUCTION

Yet each man kills the thing he loves,
By each let this be heard,
Some do it with a bitter look,
Some with a flattering word.

Oscar Wilde, The Ballad of Reading Gaol

The Reivers Way is a walking route of 150 miles around the marches of Northumberland, starting and finishing at a well-served railway station. It takes in an immense variety of scenery - soft pasture, high moorland and crags, deep shady denes, and the finest stretch of the county's coastline. It can easily be walked in nine day stages, and therefore lends itself readily to being covered all at once in a week's holiday, using the weekends at either end. An energetic walker could walk it in less: equally there is much to waylay the walker pleasantly en route, to make it worthwhile taking longer over it. The mileages given are map miles, rather than measured on the ground. There is scope for considerable variation in some of the days: you may well want to plan your own diversion or short cut.

The original guide to the Reivers Way is a small, staple bound guide written by the writer on matters Northumbrian, H.O.Wade, published in Newcastle by Frank Graham in 1977. It was originated in a contest on a programme on BBC Radio Newcastle called *To the Hills*. The winner of the contest and designer was Ken Coulson. It is he we have to thank for the Reivers Way. However, because it was Wade's word that directed me along the route initally, the text of this book refers to "Wade's route" rather than "Coulson's route".

Now, apart from the immediate vicinity of the path itself, the Reivers Way has largely been forgotten. The story of how I came to write this book is as follows.

In the centre of Newcastle upon Tyne stands a piece of true living history: if you want to have a glimpse of how your grandmother did her shopping, visit the Grainger market. You enter from Grainger Street through one of several small covered alleyways, and rather like the back of C.S.Lewis' wardrobe, you find yourself in another world. High overhead arch lofty glazed spans akin to a large railway station. Instead of platforms and destinations, different halls below are dedicated to selling different wares. In one you are assailed by greengrocers bellowing "Will that be aall noo pet?" over the hubbub: in another the rich sickly smell of cut flesh fills the air, pink and red carcases hang cheek by jowl with feathered fowls and game. In still another is a strange assortment of stalls, truly neither fish nor fowl. A cheese counter stands opposite a stall selling cheap imported suitcases and backpacks: there are hardware stalls and a petshop. The allure for the impoverished undergraduate is Robinson's book stall, selling cheap remaindered books and secondhand volumes. A winter's day early in 1982 found me there browsing as one does. I had already settled on an armful of distractions from my studies and lit upon a small book, very obviously old stock, reduced from the dizzy heights of sixty pence to a more reasonable thirty. I flicked through it, noted the maps and text in the style of a poor man's Wainwright, and that several pages had missed their appointed encounter with the printing press. How could I resist?

And that, for many years was that. I think I finished the book on the bus home and parked it in the back of my mind as something to save up for the future. I graduated, found a job and sadly like so many who received an education in that city had to head south. I left that job, went to live in Germany, returned and took a job leading trekking parties in the High Atlas mountains of Morocco. I decided, though I no longer had any base in Newcastle, that the Reivers Way would make fine preparation for the craggy Berber lands. This was in June 1989. I had three days, and thanks to plenty of energy and the long, long days, walked the route from Corbridge to Knowesgate. I was entranced, almost cursed my commitment to leaving for the dark continent. A girlfriend walked the route, and raved. During 1991 I reacquainted myself with the route on several sessions of walking. In the early summer of 1992 I rediscovered the original guide whilst clearing out my mother's house and in September of that year I set off with my bride to walk the entire route as our honeymoon.

The original route has three sections where you are walking along a route that is not indicated by the Ordnance Survey 1:50,000 mapping as having a right of way. Incitement to trespass is not something I wish to become involved in. These points will become obvious in the text - I have proposed a deviation from the original, along rights of way.

This is not a long distance path waymarked as such. A prime reason for writing a guide such as this is to persuade walkers away from such overwalked routes as the Pennine Way. The reason I have quoted Wilde's well known lines above is that I am concerned that the route should not lose its sense of exploration and isolation. How dull if one were merely to follow the same little graphic symbol for 150 miles. The Reivers Way is not recommended for the novice walker as it requires care in navigation in the lowlands and lies across pathless terrain in the hills. Nowhere will you find on the ground a sign mentioning The Reivers Way. Precisely because it is not continuously waymarked it requires a degree of competence with a 1:50,000 map and a Silva compass. The route lies along local footpaths and bridleways, some of which have become disused. In many parts it lies across stretches of trackless heather, with nothing on the ground to show that you are following a path. Respect for the environment, other people's land and our common inheritance is not just a matter of shutting gates and taking litter home. It is about being on the right path and not blundering off where you should not be. If you stray from the path on the map, the consequences of your carelessness will be felt by those who follow you.

It is difficult to say which is the best season to walk the route: I consider it to be a close run thing between June and September. Nothing can beat the colours of heather in bloom, bracken touched by the first frosts on the fells and bunches of berries glowing on the rowan trees. Nothing too, can beat the eerie ventriloquial early summer sound of snipe drumming overhead, the fizzing cry of the lapwings or woodcock roding in the dusk through the damp woods along the tributaries of the Tyne. The final two or three days, eastwards from Wooler and down the coast are perhaps at their best on clear days in midwinter, when the wide ploughlands are under frost, you look back to see the Cheviots mantled in snow, Budle Bay is full of the clamour of the greylag geese and the dunes south from Beadnell alive with wintering waders.

Whatever the season when you walk the Reivers Way, one thing is certain - that you will resolve to walk it again. There is certainly one period of the year when this route (and others in the area) should not be walked at all. From the middle of April to the middle of May the hill farms of Northumberland are going through the lambing season. However careful you are, even if you are on your own, you can still worry a skittish ewe enough for her to desert her lamb. Since the whole of the Nato training area of Otterburn ranges bans soldiers on foot, guns and aircraft for this crucial time, I think it is a small gesture for those who are privileged to use other people's land for recreation to keep away for four weeks in the year

The name "The Reivers Way" was chosen in commemoration of the raiders on both sides of the border for whom the region is so famous. The original guide explains: "The name Reivers has been chosen as being particularly appropriate to Northumbria, which, is to a greater degree than any other part of England, the land of castles, pele towers, reivers and moss-troopers and all the other concomitants of some hundreds of years of Borders warfare, sometimes official and often quite unofficial." However, the name has been made in their honour rather than attempting to follow any route supposedly taken by Border reivers. The verb "to reive" was formerly in wide usage, also spelt "reave". The *Concise Oxford Oxford Dictionary* has it thus: "Make raids, plunder; hence -er". It has a similar origin, to the verb "to rob", although the two words were quite distinct even in Anglo-Saxon. Far from the image of a mere robber, a great aura of romance now attaches itself to the Border reivers.

The Reivers Way could have been designed for the walker who wishes to study the region's wildlife. It takes you through a rich variety of habitats, many of them unique: attention is drawn to these in the text.

If you find things have changed from the text, please contact the author, care of the publishers. It only remains for me to hope that every reader will have something of the pleasure walking this route that I have enjoyed over the years.

Advice to Readers

Readers are advised that whilst every effort is taken by the author to ensure the accuracy of this guidebook, changes can occur which may affect the contents. It is advisable to check locally on transport, accommodation, shops etc but even rights-of-way can be altered and, more especially overseas, paths can be eradicated by landslip, forest fires or changes of ownership.

The publisher would welcome notes of any such changes

CORBRIDGE TO EMBLEY

CHAPTER 1
Corbridge to Allendale
17 miles

If you arrive at Corbridge station by train to start the Reivers
Way, you will find that your route takes you directly south,
away from the town. This would be a pity - Corbridge is a
fascinating and beautiful small town from which to start this
walk. As you walk up from the station the houses cluster
around the northern end of the bridge. The town itself grew
up on the crossing point on the river. The bridge was the only
one on the Tyne to survive the disastrous flood following a
great storm in 1771.

The Roman forerunner of Corbridge, Corstopitum, grew
up where Dere Street crossed the Tyne, a little upstream of
the present bridge. Nothing now remains of the Roman
bridge, although stories circulate of the stumps of piles being
visible when the water is low in summer. A wealth of old
buildings survives - a surprising number, considering the
town's turbulent history. The first Pele tower encountered on
the walk stands adjacent to St Andrew's church. Pele towers,
found on both sides of the border between England and
Scotland are small fortifications where the living quarters
were upstairs and cattle could be driven in to the ground
floor. There is another fine Pele tower at the eastern end of the
town, where the old Newcastle road enters Corbridge. It can
be seen embodied in the structure of Low Hall. At one time
St Andrew's church (damaged many times in Scottish
invasions, despite its dedication) was one of four churches in
the town. It retains some of its pre-Conquest Saxon structure.
Walk around the streets in the middle of Corbridge before

walking away from it and take time to absorb the spirit of this ancient small town, first a Roman military settlement, then a staging post on the way from Newcastle to Scotland. Nothing indicates the latter role more than the Angel Inn, a famous posting inn in its day. Reputedly Henry VIII's commissioners stayed here en route to assessing and suppressing Hexham Abbey in the 1530s. Notice the memorial sundial over the door. The Corstopitum museum, just to the west of the town, has a fine exhibition of material relating to the town's Roman past.

The Reivers Way starts at Corbridge station. In fact the best starting point is the delightful Dyvels pub, favoured watering hole of the Tynedale Rugby Club and a good introduction to the magnificent pubs to be found along the Reivers Way. The fine old stone station building, along one of the oldest railway lines in the world, has now become a smart Indian restaurant. As the road to Riding Mill crosses over the railway it makes a sharp bend to the left. Exactly on this bend you find the first footpath sign on the Reivers Way - "Mount Pleasant $^1/_2$, West Farm $1^3/_4$". It points the way up a short flight of steps, and through a small conifer plantation. You exit from this to walk uphill to cross the main Hexham-Prudhoe road, then continue due south up the hill to reach a small lane. Now turn right and follow this lane, turning right off it as the lane becomes a private drive. The path traverses the hillside, heading south west, between gorse scrub and a hedge, towards High Town Farm.

Directly below High Town is Dilston Hall - seat of the tragic Earls of Derwentwater. As the memorial stone near Langley laconically narrates "... James and Charles, Earls of Derwentwater, Viscounts Langley, beheaded on Tower Hill, 24th February 1716 and 8th December 1746, for Loyalty to their lawful sovereign". Later in the walk, we pass a spot which features in the beginnings of the Stuart dynasty on the throne of England and Scotland. The end of the Stuart dynasty came when Queen Anne died without an heir to succeed her in 1714. As James V of Scotland had predicted, referring to Mary Queen of Scots, mother of James VI of Scotland and I of England, "..it came wi' a lass and it'll gang wi' a lass". Derwentwater pledged his support for the Stuart cause and was captured in the 1715 largely Scottish rebellion. The new Hanoverian monarch turned a deaf ear to the pleas made to him by Anna, Countess of Derwentwater on bended knee, and the Third Earl was beheaded as a traitor.

Away on the far side of the valley of the Devil's Water, is Hexham levels where a battle was fought in 1464. Legends persist in the area of Margaret, the queen, escaping and being befriended by "the Hexham robber" and hiding in a cave in the woods lining the banks of the Dipton Burn. Place names still recall it - the cave is called Queen's Cave and a spot called Queen's Letch, where her horse slipped and became lame.

Keep the farm at High Town to your right and join the stony track as it follows the side of a small wood of ash and oak, climbing diagonally up the hill. The track turns to the left at the top of the wood for a few yards before turning right, away from the trees to reach the lane under a large electricity pylon. A line of thorn trees marks the route across the top of the hill. From here there is a fine view back to Tynedale and ahead to the valley of the Devil's Water. Turn right along the lane by West Farm, now sadly empty, and follow it 500 yards to a T-junction. A bridle track continues straight ahead into the trees. On your right is mature pine, the haunt of red squirrels. At intervals you can see the walls that once separated the track from what were fields on either side.

According to the map, the bridleway becomes a footpath as it nears the field in a clearing in the middle of Dipton Wood. Continue south-west down the hill, crossing the forest track, then heading down a badly eroded path to reach the cottages at GR 962 603. Walk down the hill on the hard track to reach the B6306 road. Turn right and then immediately left on a lane taking you down to Linnel Wood Farm. As you reach the farm you find a beech hedge on your right. At the end of this is a hunting gate. Go through this and head towards the dutch barn behind the farmhouse. Here a stile leads you into the field sloping down towards the woods lining the banks of the Devil's Water. You enter the woods and descend steeply on an old lane to cross the river at GR 952 597.

No footbridge is marked on the map - rest assured that there is a good footbridge here, taking you high above the water, stained to the colour of weak beer by the peaty soil upstream. Cross the bridge and take the path steeply up in the woods, here kept as a nature reserve. Now turn right along the lane in the trees and follow it for a quarter of a mile. Just before the lane leaves the woods at Ordley you find a large beech tree on your left. The path is not clearly marked here - take care. It turns left off the drive and leads through an overgrown small plantation of saplings. You walk due south and exit from the trees into a field with a small shelter for horses on its right hand side. Follow the river bank here, the new house and landscaped gardens of The Peth ahead of you, to reach Peth Foot footbridge at GR 949 589. Cross the river on this bridge and turn right on the far side of it to follow the bank along with the river on your right. After a third of a mile, walking upstream, you reach the confluence of the Devil's Water and Ham Burn. The path takes you south west, through the pine plantation and then into a field until you reach the road from Slaley to Whitley Chapel.

Turn right along the road towards Whitley Chapel for a few yards, past a pair of cottages on the right, not marked on the map. Immediately before the bridge over the Devil's Water, turn left through a wooden gate which takes you on

On the path near Embley in the valley of the Devil's Water
Hexhamshire Common

Looking northwards to Parkgates Farm
Looking towards Staward from Jingle Pot

Looking north along the valley of Devil's Water from Embley

to a good track, heading south west along the wooded bank of the river. You pass the ruins of an old smelt mill (not shown on the map) dating from the days when Allendale was a lead mining centre, and then exit from the woods just after the footbridge marked on the map at GR 936 577. This footbridge leads to a path taking you up to Whitley Chapel and the Fox and Hounds pub. In fact there is a valid short cut from the original Reivers Way, taking some little-used paths from Whitley Chapel village via Aydon Shields, Salmon Field, Rowley Head, Gair Shield and then straight over Burntridge Moor to High Struthers and Allendale.

The Reivers Way proper is now on a faint track running southwards across the pasture, bringing you to the empty cottage at GR 931 574. According to the map, the right of way takes you away from the track, to the left, south-east up the hill to Steel Hall. In fact there is no sign of this on the ground and it is fairly obvious that the right of way now continues

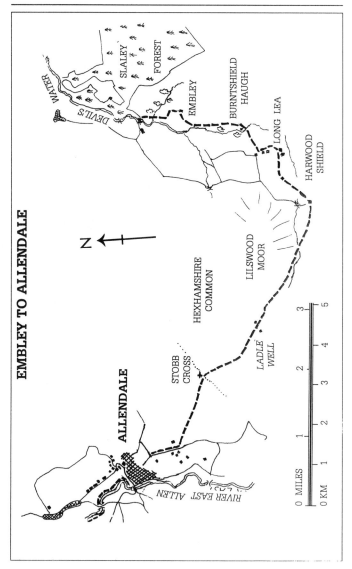

EMBLEY TO ALLENDALE

southwards to reach the crossroads at GR 930 560. The Reivers Way here follows the public road for a third of a mile, down the hill until the road makes a small hairpin to the right at a slightly strange rural traffic island, just before crossing back over the Devil's Water at GR 927 557. Turn left here along the drive to Embley Farm, southwards to cross the Apperley Burn and enter the woods. Ignore the small footbridge over the Devil's Water at its confluence with the Apperley Burn.

The track turns to the left as it leaves the wood and goes up the hill to reach the farm on top of the hill. From the farm buildings a lane runs due south, not marked on the map. Immediately after the farm turn right off this, through a gate, to follow the barely discernible bridleway which takes you diagonally down across the gorse-covered slope to reach the Devil's Water in its wooded dene. You enter the trees and walk along the bank to a ford taking a farm lane south west to Broadwell House. Leave this behind you as you continue southwards, crossing another unnamed tributary, the river now dwindling as you near its source. Ahead of you now are the heather-covered slopes of Redburn Moor: the Reivers Way is now near the transition of the Devil's Water from moorland burn to woodland stream.

Cross the river at the farm at Burntshield Haugh, following the farm lane up the hill towards Hesleywell. The lane takes a right-angle right hand bend at a patch of thistles and nettles, whilst the footpath keeps straight on over a stile. Ahead of you on the skyline you see three houses, from left to right New House, Hesleywell and Loaming House. Make for the middle one with the prominent asbestos farm buildings and turn left at the house to traverse along the slope before passing to the right of the scanty remains of the cottage at GR 919 524. The path now lies diagonally down the hill to the chicken sheds at Long Lee. For this stretch the Reivers Way is not waymarked: its route is marked by stiles and gates.

The bridle-way as marked on the map from Long Lee to Stobby Lea, via Steel Grove (wrongly named "Steel" on the map) is effectively impossible to follow. A more direct route, slightly to the south of what is marked on the map is the best course. At Stobby Lea you should keep the house on your left as you run the gauntlet of snapping collies. At the far side of the farm you see a small garage building: keep this and the fence beyond it to your right as you follow the bridle track south west, diagonally down the hill to the corner of the field. Here is a step stile with a triangular warning sign about the bull, followed by a rudimentary footbridge taking you across the Stobbylee Burn. You are now on rough grazing as you head south west up the slope to Harwood Shield Farm in a small grove of trees. Walk through the farmyard, turn left along the hard track for a few yards, and then immediately right, along the track heading due west onto Hexhamshire Common.

Thus far, the day's walk has taken you from the Tyne itself, little more than ten miles upstream of its highest tidal point at Wylam, through a scene changing from lowland arable fields and deciduous woods to upland sheep farms. For the next four miles you are among moorland, haunt of grouse and curlew and little different in appearance from Arctic tundra.

After two thirds of a mile you come to a bend in the track marked on the map (GR 896 515). Turn right here onto a grassy track which descends to meet a gate near the culvert over the Stobbylea Burn. You now ascend the slope of Hangman Hill, following a new (1992) Land Rover track of rubble and gravel. In fact this does not exactly follow the line of the bridleway, taking you well to the north of the saddle between Pikeley Rigg and Lilswood Moor. You reach a junction of tracks in the heather (approx GR 890 523). Turn left here - you can see the old railway wagons and corrugated iron shooting hut at Ladle Well ahead of you. You cross the Linn Burn on an old stone bridge at its confluence with the Black Sike. In late summer beehives are placed here for the bees to gather the precious nectar and pollen of the heather. The track junction at GR 876 526 is just as the map marks it: keep to the right of the Linn Burn here on a narrow path through the heather.

Away to the north, on your right hand side as you walk, are views to Tynedale and the moors and forests beyond. Over your right hand shoulder you can see Dipton Wood, walked through just a few hours before. Stobb Cross, at 1326ft is the highest point reached today and is embellished with a fine wooden signpost, a growing cairn at its foot. Shortly after this the bridleway across the moor becomes an enclosed track as it descends towards the road. You turn right onto the public road at GR 846 546 and this little-used public road takes you steeply down into Allendale. The village itself is concealed until the final mile of the day: on a still evening the smoke from the town's hearths rises and settles in a haze over the roofs.

The centre of Allendale is built around a large green, crossed by several roads. In the centre of this open space is a group of shops, including an excellent grocer's open every evening until ten o'clock. Outside the grocer's the buses to Alston and Hexham stop. To sample all the pubs in Allendale, vying with each other with their sandwich boards and window announcements, would probably do more than anaesthetize the feet from the battering received along the way from Corbridge.

The farms around Allendale tend to be much smaller than found elsewhere on the walk - formerly they were owned by farmer-miners who combined part-time farming with working the lead seams of Allendale. The town itself is well known for its New Year festival that has origins in an era long before the conversion of Northumberland to Christianity. A great bonfire is lit in the square and men with blackened faces - "guisers" approach with barrels of blazing tar on their heads. In Lerwick in Shetland is a very similar ceremony, generally believed to have Viking origins. There are almost no Scandinavian place names around Allendale, however and it lies to the north of the Danelaw negotiated by King Alfred. Other New Year traditions are shared with Scotland, such as first footing - a dark man bearing salt, coal and money, knocking at the door and being welcomed inside with generally liquid refreshments.

CHAPTER 2
Allendale to Bardon Mill
11 miles

This is a short day's walk, giving the walker time to visit the Roman fort at Vindolanda and Housesteads. Although the day stage finishes at the High Street of Bardon Mill, the most attractive way of walking the route would no doubt be to continue a little further and stay overnight above Tynedale: bed and breakfast is offered at many houses and farms on or near the Reivers Way - there are also hotels and the Youth Hostel at Once and Twice Brewed. All these are listed, with grid references to find them on the map, in the Appendix.

Leave Allendale past the Hare and Hounds pub, descending a short hill. As the road describes a left hand bend you will find a footpath doubling back to the right below a railing. A sign points the way to "Allenmill ³/₄, Oakpool 2³/₄". You pass a garden on your left hand side and walk downstream along the banks of the river. In the woods you find a footbridge and a ruined mine entrance from which a stream exits from a dungeon-like grating. Out of the woods the path runs through pasture along the banks of the river, where alder trees arch over the water. After two thirds of a mile you reach the B road where it crosses the river, where you turn left to cross the bridge.

Immediately over the bridge, turn right at a sign saying "Oakpool 2 miles" and continue to follow the Allen downstream, now on the west bank. You leave the woods and follow a waymarked path over the meadows of the alluvial plain of the Allen. Just over half a mile later you reach an empty cottage and caravan (GR 817 573). It seems that the

ALLENDALE TO BARDON MILL

last occupier here diverted the path away from his precious cottage. The path continues along the bank, the Allen now a gentler, more mature river than the stony stream just two miles above at Allendale Town. You climb a stile to re-enter the woods and cross Maggies Bridge, erected in 1983. After a quarter of a mile of woods you find yourself at the fields around Kiddy Green, where the present owners seem to prefer to live in a caravan than the house itself. The drive now takes you to Oakpool Farm, where you meet the public road. Turn left along this road, initially with the river on your right, and then walk uphill away from the river in the woods. Half a mile after the bridge you come to a right hand turning and a footpath sign indicating Hindley Hill Farm and Wide Eals.

Follow this lane, with the conifer plantation on the right, to Hindley Hill Farm. Beyond the farm the path is less easy to follow, being little used. Follow it through several gates, then steeply down the hill to the bridge over the River Allen at Wide Eals Farm. The farm drive now takes you obliquely up the hill to meet the main A686 road at the hairpin bend above the Cupola Bridge. In the trees below you to your left is the confluence of the Rivers East and West Allen. Turn left on the main road to follow it 600 yards to the bridge. Just before the bridge turn right to take the path, initially along the banks and then steeply up through the woods. You leave the woods to find yourself in a grazing field well supplied with bracken and ragwort - follow the left hand side of the field to meet the main road at a ladder stile and signpost.

Turn left on the main road and follow it along for a few hundred yards to the former Staward Station on the old Hexham to Allendale branch line. The road from Catton meets the main road at two points as it descends the former railway embankment. Opposite the second turning, by the old station buildings, you turn left through a farm gate set back from the road and walk along a rutted track twisting northwards across the fields. After two gates you come to Gingle Pot ruin, a former inn serving cattle drovers. Here you find a stone wall running directly away from you to the north. The path lies to the left of this, a green stripe through the weedy fields. It takes you to the edge of the wood where a yellow arrow and a stile at an enormous stone gatepost marks the path to Harsondale (GR 804 606). Here the path following the old drovers road can be seen, a faint line curving across the fields following a line of oak trees, then to enter the wood and descend to the base of the Allen Valley. Here the map is a little at variance with what you find on the ground.

Directly to the west of where you are standing a footpath enters the woods at a prominent cottage-loaf shaped National Trust sign announcing Staward Gorge (GR 803 606). Follow the footpath to this, over the stile and into the woods. You are now following what Wade calls "a narrow and natural causeway to the scrub and tree-covered summit of the crag". It is actually more than this - a narrow spur in the woods almost 300 feet high, formed by the confluence of the Allen and Staward Burn. On the way to Staward Pele you find gaps in the trees, giving magnificent views of the sparkling Allen as it makes its way through a deep ravine. Suddenly you come upon the remains of a wall in the woods, then Staward Pele itself. It stands in a strategic, not to say dramatic position, scarcely diminished now by being overgrown with ivy and sycamore trees. It is first mentioned as being the gift of the Duke of York in 1386 to the friars of Hexham Abbey, although it had certainly been in existence for some time before then. At the Dissolution it passed to the crown. The Pele was locally famous in the nineteenth century as the scene of picnics which were held here in the field nearby.

From the Pele a steep and rocky path returns you to the river where an old wooden footbridge takes you over the

Staward Burn, then northward along the bank of the Allen in the woods. Cypher's Linn is a reputedly bottomless pool along this stretch, to which attaches itself a tale of buried treasure. There is a story of a man bringing a team of oxen with ropes to haul out a chest, supposedly hidden by the monks from Hexham Abbey on departure from the Pele. His only reward was for the entire assemblage to fall in to the river and take him with it. The River Allen keeps its secret as it makes its way among the trees. Take care along this stretch as you make your way above the often sheer banks of the river.

Below Hag Bank is one of the finest stretches of the river. It is effectively now in a gorge: across the stream can be seen exposed strata of carboniferous limestone, sandstone and shales. The most exciting inhabitant of this stretch is the otter, which you are highly unlikely to see. You will however find dippers, sandpipers, wagtails and the occasional kingfisher. You leave the woods at a fork where the Reivers Way takes you to the left, along a bridle path into the fields at Plankey Mill. This is a campsite and beauty spot popular with locals in the summer. An ancient sign nailed to the tree as you approach the farm announces Wall's ice cream. Of more interest is a tent cooking bacon sandwiches and all day breakfasts. We sat in the sunshine and ordered steaming mugs of tea, loaves of toast and squadrons of sausages. All was served with admiring comments on the distance we had walked and size of our rucksacks.

Turn left at Plankey Mill to cross the river on a suspension bridge. Turn right immediately over the bridge to cross the Kingswood Burn and enter Briarwood Banks nature reserve. This is a stretch of natural woodland which has remained undisturbed since the last Ice Age. It therefore represents the climatic climax vegetation for the locality. There are nineteen species of native trees in the woods, among them oak, lime,

The footbridge at Plankey Mill. Photo: W.Unsworth

willows, sallow, whitebeam, yew and alder. It is a precious habitat indeed. Walk through these woods and follow the River Allen downstream, now into the National Trust property of Allen Banks. A mile after Plankey Mill the path forks: take the left hand path up the hill. The right hand path goes over the footbridge, marked on the map. At the end of the wood you are looking north west to Ridley Hall. Do not double back up the path in the trees here (not marked on the map), but go through the gate on the left and follow the ha-ha along the edge of the parkland.

Ridley Hall was once the home of the Lords Ridley. The most famous of the clan was Nicholas Ridley, one of the Oxford Martyrs, around whose monument the traffic grinds, overlooked by the Randolph Hotel in the centre of Oxford. Together with Bishop Latimer he was put to death for his Protestant faith in October 1555, just three years before the death of the Catholic Mary Tudor. Latimer encouraged Ridley at the point of death with the famous words: "Be of good comfort, Master Ridley and play the man - we shall this day light such a candle in England, as by God's grace shall never be put out."

The spot where Ridley met his death has changed much: all that he would recognise now is the front of Balliol College. In contrast, the area immediately around where he grew up has changed but little. The Ridley family lost their lands, not through supporting the Stuarts in 1715 or 1745, but in the preceding century, during the Civil War of Charles I. Now the Hall is a college, although the family name lives on - for a time one Nicholas Ridley served in Margaret Thatcher's cabinet and was rewarded with a peerage.

Turn left when you meet the road, then almost immediately right at the telephone box to the almost too-perfect hamlet of Beltingham, with its Saxon church much restored in the nineteenth century. Follow the road along as it passes the wood on the right. This is now Beltingham nature reserve, established because of the unique flora thriving on soils affected by the high metallic content of silt washed from the mines of the North Pennines. Species found in the woods include various vetches, marsh marigolds, wild thyme and mountain pansy. Turn right just after the trees to cross the river on a rusty footbridge into Bardon Mill. There is a right of way here for vehicles to ford the river, although this is no longer passable. (From Ridley Hall Wade's original route ran down the road to Ridley Bridge and then along the busy A69 trunk road from Newcastle to Carlisle.) Cross the railway at the level crossing just after the campsite and walk up to the war memorial by the old main road, now mercifully by-passed. The centre of Bardon Mill village lies to your left.

CHAPTER 3
Bardon Mill to Wark via Hadrian's Wall
13 miles

The feature which dominates today's walk is Hadrian's Wall, although only two miles are spent walking on the wall itself. It is the finest remaining Roman structure in Britain and has caused much spillage of ink since being studied by antiquarians from the nineteenth century onwards. Unlike so many archeological remains it is easy to see exactly what it was built for - to stand on its ramparts and contemplate the enormous mass of the Roman empire behind you and the lawless lands to the north gives a deep impression of the might of Rome.

Contrary to popular opinion, it was not Julius Caesar who conquered Britain. In 54 and 55 BC he made two reconnaissance expeditions to the hinterland of the south coast of England. He was nearing completion of his conquest of Gaul - roughly modern day France. At this time the population on either side of the channel and western North Sea were of the same stock - closely allied Celtic tribes. It is important to bear in mind that "England" did not exist - the population of southern Britain were speaking a language from which modern Welsh was derived. Caesar found that the presence of unconquered Britain across the Channel had an unsettling effect on the subject population of northern Gaul. His assassination in 44 BC precipated a struggle for control of the territories of Rome and the creation of a hereditary Empire in a bid to promote stability, replacing the

BARDON MILL TO WARK

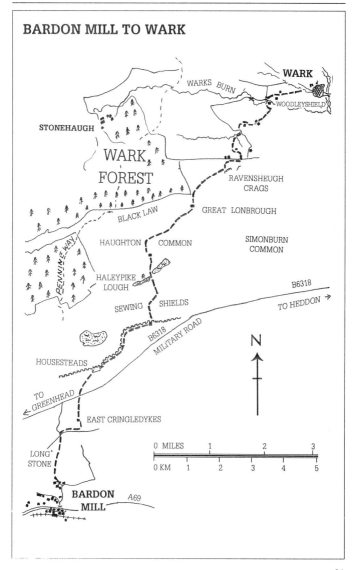

WARK

WARKS BURN

WOODLEYSHIELD

STONEHAUGH

WARK FOREST

RAVENSHEUGH CRAGS

GREAT LONBROUGH

BLACK LAW

SIMONBURN COMMON

HAUGHTON COMMON

PENNINE WAY

HALEYPIKE LOUGH

B6318

TO HEDDON →

SEWING SHIELDS

B6318

MILITARY ROAD

N

HOUSESTEADS

TO GREENHEAD ←

EAST CRINGLEDYKES

LONG STONE

BARDON MILL

A69

0 MILES 1 2 3

0 KM 1 2 3 4 5

former republic. Caesar's nephew Augustus became the first Emperor in 27 BC, whose throne eventually passed to Claudius, on the death of the mad Caligula in the year AD 41.

Claudius was a descendant of Caesar and it was he who set out to follow Caesar's visit with a full-scale invasion in AD 43. Lustre was added to the campaign by the arrival of the Emperor himself to take control of the forces in the first year of Roman occupation. Roman control of Britain slowly expanded from the south-east until the summer of AD 61 when a summer of campaigning in North Wales against the Ordovices was interrupted by a revolt of the Iceni in what is now East Anglia, under their Queen Boadicea. During this uprising the Ninth Legion, garrisoned at Lincoln, was defeated. At this time, the northern frontier was not fixed, but based on a series of legionary bases (a legion was a body of troops roughly equivalent to a modern division), at Caerleon, Chester and York. This was changed, following the appointment of Agricola as governor of Britain in the year 78. Events during his time in office are well recorded by his son in law, Tacitus, famous as the writer of *Germania*, and as biographer of Agricola. One of the new governor's first acts was to secure his northern front on a line of forts slightly to the south of what was to become Hadrian's Wall.

This was Stanegate, a Roman road starting at Carlisle and ending at Corbridge - there is no evidence of it continuing further east. The defensive line of the Stanegate forts (Vindolanda was originally just one of these, as was Corbridge itself) anticipated the building of Hadrian's Wall by some forty years. In the year 81 Agricola advanced further, and established forts along the Forth-Clyde line, which became sixty years later, the Antonine Wall. Three years later, he defeated the Highland tribes at the battle of Mons Graupius

The River Allen at Plankey Bridge. Photo: W.Unsworth

View eastwards from the earthworks at Manside Cross

Hadrian's Wall at Housesteads gives magnificent walking
(Photo: R.B.Evans)

in the vicinity of Inverness. A few months after (in the winter of 84-5) Agricola was recalled to Rome. The "what if?" school of historical study is a fool's game indeed, but it is tempting to consider that, given a few more summers' campaigning, Agricola would have secured all of the British mainland and thereby rendered the building of Hadrian's Wall unnecessary. Without the pen of Tacitus to enlighten us, comparatively little is known of the intervening forty years between the departure of Agricola and the accession of Hadrian to the emperor's throne in AD 117. At this time, the northern frontier of Rome was on the line of the Stanegate forts: the evidence is that problems elsewhere on the Empire's frontiers bled troops away from Britain and therefore a partial withdrawal from areas difficult to control, such as the mountains of Caledonia. During this time some British troops were serving the empire in Dacia, modern Romania - later some Dacian cohorts were to garrison the Wall itself. Two millennia later I found myself walking the wall with my Romanian wife.

In the year 122 the Emperor Hadrian visited Britain: his policy was one of consolidation rather than conquest and accordingly he ordered the building of the wall that bears his name, to secure his northern front. It was complete by the year 130. In 138 Hadrian died and, following the accession of Antonius to the imperial throne, plans were made for expansion of the empire into Scotland. The result was the building of the Antonine Wall, from Kilpatrick on the Clyde, to Carriden, near Bo'ness on the Firth of Forth and until the end of the second century, the empire's northernmost boundary moved several times between the two lines. In 181 Hadrian's Wall was breached, as the effect of unstable leadership from Rome began to be felt on its frontiers. There was a further rebellion in 197: nine years later the emperor Severus arrived in Britain to spend the next three years campaigning in Northern Britain until his death at Eboracum, York in 211. Thus for this period the Wall was only sporadically garrisoned as a fixed frontier.

For the rest of the century the wall appears to have fulfilled its intended role, until Britain began to be involved in the internal struggles that became the death throes of the Roman Empire. Carausius ruled Britain from 286 to 293 and claimed to be emperor too. For whatever reason, considerable rebuilding took place during this time. For much of the fourth century, as power steadily devolved in the Empire, the wall remained as its northern border. There was an invasion in 343, which precipitated the visit of Emperor Constans, son of Constantine the Great who ruled the empire from present day Istanbul. Under Constantine's rule Christianity took hold in this country for the first time. This was a prelude to the great attacks of 367, when Roman Britain was invaded from the north, by the Caledonian tribes, from Ireland in the west and most significantly, from across the North Sea by the tribes inhabiting the coastal areas of what is now Germany and the Netherlands, speaking a language which developed into English. It took two years for this invasion and rebellion to be quelled, and for the frontier to be returned to Hadrian's Wall. In fact the reconquest of the province, under Theodosius, father of the emperor of that name, was just a temporary repreive for Roman rule in Britain.

The year 383 is generally held as being the last in which Hadrian's Wall was occupied. At this time the province was continually providing a springboard for bids to claim the imperial throne. Each contender who attempted to take over the western empire took troops with him from Britain and thus weakened the empire here. In fact there is no clear date for the end of Roman rule: the picture is of power devolving to local Romano-British leaders, and increasing threat of wholesale invasion from across the North Sea. In the year 410 all ties were finally cut between Britain and what remained of the Roman Empire, the Anglo-Saxon invasion began in earnest and Christianity began its retreat into the margins of the north and west. Two and a quarter centuries later we find a monk from just such a fastness, Iona, invited by the Angle king of Northumbria, Oswald, to preach in his kingdom. The year was 634, the monk's name was Aidan and he chose the Farne Islands, encountered later on the Reivers Way, as his base.

The popular conception of Hadrian's Wall is that it was built and served as a defensive barrier until the demise of the Roman Empire. Its history was a little more complex than this. In fact the wall was not intended as a defensive feature. At regular intervals are gatehouses, giving access through the wall. The Roman army excelled in rapid manoeuvre and close-quarter fighting in infantry squares by well-drilled troops. The wall was used as a base for just such tactics, in combination with forward outposts to the north of the wall. What it did serve as, was a visible barrier - a clear boundary line, south of which *Pax Romana* held sway.

Let us set forth from Bardon Mill to discover Hadrian's Wall for itself. Cross over the old main road by the war memorial and take the lane under the main road, whereupon you come to a fork. Turn left here and after 300 yards turn right at a left hand bend to walk steeply up the hill towards Westend Town. Turn right on the farm lane then left to walk due north up the hill to pass under the pylon line. A quarter of a mile after the pylons you turn right off the farm track at the corner of a small copse to continue north. The path takes you over Barcombe Down (not named on the map), between the stone pillar "Long Stone" and the trig point. Stone was quarried from this hill to make the Roman wall.

From the summit of Barcombe Down there is a fine view

of the area of the wall and particularly of Vindolanda fort. The first Northumbrian Lough comes into view - Grindon Lough. In fact this appears to have been wrongly named by the Ordnance Survey - strictly it should be Beamwham Lough. There is also a good view down to Vindolanda Roman fort. In the summer of 1992 Vindolanda hit the headlines with the revelation that at long last the emperor Hadrian's headquarters whilst building the wall had been discovered. It was a four-sided edifice with more than fifty rooms, a central cobbled courtyard and oak walls up to fifty yards long. There were frescoes of men with beards - a style introduced to the Empire by Hadrian himself. Vindolanda would have been a natural choice for the headquarters as it was a Stanegate fort, preceding the construction of the wall, and lies half way along the wall's length of eighty Roman miles.

Chesterholm Roman fort - Vindolanda - makes a very worthwhile diversion from the Reivers Way. It is open daily from February to November: there are large preserved excavations of the fort and civilian settlement - *vicus* - and a fine museum with commentaries, explaining life on the Wall. A wall turret has been entirely reconstructed as part of the display. To reach Vindolanda, turn left when you meet the road at GR781 669, then right at the turning half a mile later to cross the Brackies Burn. To rejoin the Reivers Way walk westwards along the tarred public road that follows the Roman Stanegate, then turn left over the cattle grid to take you along the drive to East Crindledykes Farm. To the west of the farm lane is a quarry for the limestone where good geological folding is revealed, also several lime-loving plant species - burnet, thyme and cowslips - unusual in this area of largely igneous geology. Keep the farm to your left and head across the grazing fields to join the Military Road. To your right is the limestone outcrop of Green Brae, not named on the map. As you join the Military Road you find yourself opposite the lane to Housesteads Farm, rather than as the map shows.

This road, running as straight as an arrow to the north of Tyne valley, is known as the Military Road, or just plain "the Military" to the locals. It's name does not originate, as one might surmise, from the Roman soldiers who built it, but from the aftermath of the 1715 Scottish rebellion against the Hanoverian monarchy. General Wade, famous for his network of roads built to move Hanoverian troops through the Highlands, had the road built to replace the poor roads connecting Newcastle and Carlisle. In many places it lies actually on the wall itself. At Twice Brewed he sampled the beer at an inn and, not being satisfied, ordered the landlord to brew it again - hence the name. The youth hostel was named Once Brewed as something of a joke.

Take the farm road past Housesteads farm to the museum and fine remains of the wall fort of Vercovicium. Between the Military Road and the farm you can see the lynchets, terraces and strip fields marking the ground where marginal land was cultivated for crops in the twelfth and thirteenth centuries. Housesteads is simply one of the finest Roman sites in the country. The small museum is open daily all year round. The information sheet issued by the local tourist office boasts of Housesteads having "the finest Roman latrine in Britain". A footpath runs from the eastern side of the excavated Roman encampment. You leave the museum area through a gate and walk on the south side of the wall, down the hill to the crossing of the Knag Burn. From the bridge you continue on the south side of the wall, now going uphill towards a plantation. You cross a stile, walk through the copse and leave it over another stile. You now continue to follow the wall as it takes you over Kings Hill and Clew Hill and past Busy Gap, a broad gap in the ridge followed by Hadrian's

Wall. This was a spot much frequented by moss troopers and border reivers. When Camden and Cotton visited the area in 1599 they were advised to avoid this stretch of the extant Roman Wall. The term of mild abuse "a Busy Gap Rogue" persisted in use until the seventeenth century. (None of these three features are named on the 1:50,000 map.)

Half a mile after the trig point on Sewingshields Crags you come to the small ancient wood surrounding Sewingshields Farm, where you can find excellent bed and breakfast accommodation (see Appendix). The legend persists in the locality of a shepherd sitting on top of the crags in the trees near the farm, doing his knitting. He dropped his clew - needle - with wool attached and followed it down the cliff face. It led him to a cave entrance, where upon entering he made his way inside to find a lit chamber and King Arthur and his knights in residence. The present incumbents at the farm recount their sons' attempts to find this cave entrance. In the hall of the farmhouse is a namestone commemorating the centurion Gellius Philipus. From the farm you will see a hard farm track running away to the north from the foot of Sewingshields crags. Walk through the farm and turn left onto this track. A glance behind you will reveal the low granite escarpment of the Whin Sill. A little over a mile and a half of walking along this easy track, now grassed over in places, brings you to the farm at Stell Green, GR 807 723.

This is the first instance of Wade's Reivers Way straying from a clear right of way. He directs the walker northwards along the footpath that follows the unsurfaced farm track northwards to the small farm of Stell Green. ".... shortly after, Haleypike Lough appears on the right, the path passing between them. ... At the next farm, apparently deserted, the track ends. Head for a crag a little to north from where a small hill with sheep-folds can be seen to the north east: head for this and from the sheep-folds Lonbrough Farm will be seen..."

We have here a curious case of a footpath right of way finishing in the middle of nowhere, at the farm.

Here in a nutshell you have a classic example of the puzzles besetting the cartographer, responsible walker, landowner and indeed writer of walking guides. The directions for the original Reivers Way clearly direct the walker along a direct route from Stell Green to Great Lonbrough. Indeed old Bartholomew mapping shows such a path, connecting at Great Lonbrough with the path running south-west to north-east across Haughton Common. The original compilers of the Ordnance Survey mapping did not start with a *tabula rasa* for rights of way. Footpaths are based on older records. In many other instances one can find a footpath marked on the map finishing in the middle of nowhere at a parish boundary because in the year dot, one parish clerk was more diligent than another in marking footpaths. Consider the case of this path: what ever use is a public path if it follows a farm track from the road to a farm, with no right of way leading from the farm at all? It would seem that in practice there is a right of way continuing beyond Stell Green, but to suggest that this exists on the ground without being marked by the Ordnance Survey is to unlock a Pandora's box best left well sealed. I have found no objection raised in the past to my crossing this particular stretch. Always ask before you walk. In 1992, the National Park Authorities were studying the claim that there was indeed a footpath north-east from Stell Green, as it seems that there should be. If you ask, or better still, stay at Sewingshields Farm, you will be given permission to walk north beyond Stell Green in the morning.

There is an alternative route, following the Pennine Way northwards from a point on the wall just to the west of Housesteads, GR 781 686. A mile and a half north of the wall you enter a southern salient of the huge Wark Forest, on a

39

track. After 400 yards a footpath branches off on the right. If you miss this - easily done - continue a further 600 yards down the hill towards the Haughton Green Burn. Turn right along the south bank to reach Haughton Green and then head north east to emerge from the forest onto Haughton Common.

Whether approached from the south or west, Haughton Common is a featureless expanse of heather, cotton grass, tussocks and rough grazing. Here you really test your navigation. To a novice map reader, contours are often a forgotten background to easier features such as road junctions and buildings. To the seasoned navigator contours are all. On Haughton Common they really are all you have. From Stell Green to Great Lonbrough there is little or no evidence of the path on the ground, so study the contours and follow the course of the path as it makes its way across the almost imperceptible watershed between the Sell Burn and the Hopeshield Burn. On the right hand side of Stell Green you find a gate in a fence marked with a National Park badge. From here walk 300 metres north, crossing the tiny Sell Burn. You are now on the footpath running from Haughtongreen to Great Lonbrough, although it is barely discernible on the ground. Turn right now and use your compass to bring you 400 yards later to the gate and bend in the Sell Burn (GR 810 728). The prominent ridge to your right has, at its highest point, Townshield Bank, GR 817 729. Here are peat hags facing to the north, a useful navigation feature. Having jumped across the Sell Burn, use your compass to take you to the top of a low hill where you find a prominent stone sheep fold. This involves crossing a sponge-like mass of peat. By the time you reach the sheep fold Great Lonbrough Farm has come into sight, and the rutted track approaching it. Walk across the front of the farm, leaving the buildings to your left and pass through two gates to continue along the drive, past

Ravensheugh Crags to the road at a pale brown portakabin house.

One has the sense that Wade was tired as he neared the end of his day at Wark. ".. the footpaths across this final stretch, some two to three miles, cannot any longer be found and there is no certainty that the stiles will be there." Yes, the lanes are pleasant, but the approach to Wark is infinitely finer if made along the paths, which, though largely now abandoned, can still be found. Turn right to head east along the road to the drive to Catless Farm with its prominent red barn doors. Turn left here and walk down to the farm. Immediately in front of the farm turn left across the field in front of the house, keeping it to your right. You go through a gate then turn right to walk down the slope with a small stand of conifers on your right. At the bottom of this is a dry stone wall with a step stile in it, now little used. Cross over this stile into a field of rough grazing (in the reverse of the usual case, you walk downhill to leave hay meadow and find yourself among tussock grass) and now descend steeply to the Gofton burn. Turn right to cross the tributary stream and follow the southern bank of the Gofton Burn along to the road at a pile of gravel. Turn left over the bridge, then immediately right after crossing the stream. You walk through a gate by the post box for the cottage in front of you. Keep the cottage on your left and walk along the faint track through the grass along the side of the Gofton Burn, before slanting up the hillside towards the copse at High Moralee.

Two paths cross Moralee Bank, heading north east, one from High Moralee, the other from the cottage up the river. However both of these have been fenced across: they are legitimate footpaths now sadly ignored. You are well within your rights to follow them, but will have to climb several fences now to do so. To avoid this, follow the drive from High Moralee back across the river and to the public road. Turn left along the road to cross back to the north side of the Gofton Burn. The road climbs steeply for a short distance, as it approaches Low Moralee farm. Now take care with your navigation, because the paths are not waymarked on the ground. As you walk up the hill along the road, there is a stone wall on your left. You reach the top of a slope and pass under a cable just before the farm buildings at Low Moralee. Turn left through a gateway (GR 846 762) and follow the track to the north. It is marked on the map as a black, pecked line. You now find yourself following a line of electricity pylons and are walking on a prominent track. As this track starts to drop down into the valley of the Wark Burn it swings to the left, following an ancient avenue of oak trees. A sunken, muddy lane in a field, it brings you to a delightful old mill where you join a road over a bridge. Immediately after the bridge at the old mill you find a set of stone steps on your right. Climb these and walk across the field to join the drive to Woodley Shield. Keep Woodley Shield on your right and walk up the hill to the new barn at GR 847 770. The path now takes you along the right hand side of two arable fields, then down the hill and across the Dean Burn into Wark.

You may have noticed, if chatting to the locals, that "Wark" is pronounced to rhyme with "shark" or "bark". The village is often called Wark-on-Tyne, to distinguish it from the other village of Wark, on the River Tweed, long fought over as a border castle. Two miles to the south-east is Chipchase Castle, not open to the public. In mediaeval times, Wark was the capital of North Tynedale. Now you can find refreshment at the Grey or the Black Bulls, ancient hostels both, or the rather smarter Battlesteads Hotel on the Simonburn road (see Appendix). The village grocer closed in 1991, its place being taken by the shop attached to the garage in the centre of the village.

CHAPTER 4
Wark to Elsdon
18 miles

Leave the village over the girder bridge crossing the North Tyne. At the end of the bridge is a T-junction: the main road turns right to run past Chipchase castle to Chollerford. Instead turn left and immediately afterwards turn right at a bungalow to go uphill, keeping on the road. Turn right again at a T-junction after a few yards and follow this road as it goes over the bridge crossing the old North Tyne railway line. The road goes steeply up, and round a sharp right hand bend, past a turning to the right without a signpost. You enter a small wood as you cross a stream. Shortly afterwards you come to a large wooden gate set back from the road. You are looking uphill at a pine wood. Turn left through the gate and walk up to this and along its left hand edge over a ridge. You then drop down to an ancient ladder stile and minute footbridge. Keep straight ahead up the hill. At the top of the hill you see the houses of Birtley. On the left hand side of these, beneath three birch trees, is a stile and path along the side of a garden that takes you up to Birtley Church and war memorial. Turn left and walk through the village. Here is a parish that obviously goes to great lengths to succeed in best kept village competitions - even the sign announcing the entrance to the village has a flower bed around its base.

Keep up the hill through the village, past a sign for Birtley Shields and walk up to a fork in the road. Turn left here and after a quarter of a mile you will see a tall ladder stile on your right. As you stand on top of it, look ahead across a field

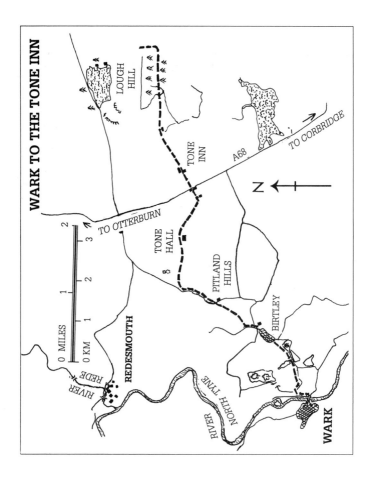

Mediaeval strip fields near Birtley

much ridged with mediaeval strip fields to the house at Pittland Hill. Walk straight ahead to this, passing through a couple of gates. Turn left on the road and follow it due north, over a cattle grid and past the farm at Lowshield Green. Shortly after the farm you walk round a right hand bend in the road with a walled in field on your right hand side. Notice how the map faithfully marks where the road has a hedge or wall lining it, and on which side. At the end of the field on your right, turn right across the tussocky grass, following the faint line of the old bridleway. Away to your left is a hut near where the cairn is marked on the map. In early summer the air is full of the eerie sound of snipe drumming overhead. The right of way is marked by a hunting gate in a stone wall before reaching the trees around Tone Hall. The hard track that takes you through the rather manorial farm at Tone Hall is exactly as marked on the map.

From the front of Tone Hall walk south west along the

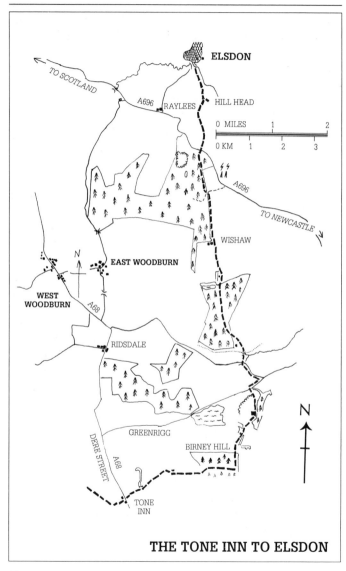

THE TONE INN TO ELSDON

driveway to the Tone Inn (GR 914 801). This makes a suitable lunchtime halt, a watering hole for travellers along the lonely A68 Dere Street as it makes it switchback route towards Otterburn and on to Scotland. Traffic moves very fast past the Tone Inn and there is dangerous dead ground to the north: take special care in crossing the road. Opposite the road from the Tone Inn you will see a step stile in the stone wall. Climb this and walk across to join the drive as it takes you through Whiteside to White House. A mile to the north is the open area of rough grass known as Green Rigg, looked over by Wanney Crags. It is a barren spot: here in October 1715 the levies from Northumbria gathered to support "James III" and marched north to proclaim him king in Rothbury. By the year's end the little army was scattered, many of Northumberland's nobility and gentry dead and the Hanoverian monarch more firmly on the throne.

From White House a footpath is marked on the map heading due east, but Wade plotted a route northwards over Cowstand Hill. Whenever I have asked, I have been allowed to walk this route, but it is not a right of way. Instead, keep heading due east from White House, to cross the tiny Reed Sike stream. Be warned that the plantation on Birney Hill has been extended to the south: the marking of the forest on the map bears little relation to what you find on the ground. In fact the footpath has been sensibly diverted to follow the stone wall that marks the southern edge of the woods as shown on the map. Sadly it is little used. You cross the Reed Sike Burn at GR 937 809 and bear left to follow the wall due east for almost a mile until you come to a gate in the wall almost at the end of the plantation. Turn left through this and head along the track to the north. This junction is exactly on the join of map sheets 80 and 81. Head uphill across the field, the left hand side of a narrow pine copse ahead and walk along the side of this to reach a track junction at a sheep shed and ruined dutch barn at GR 951 820. From here turn right and head north east along a track to the barn at GR 955 826.

At the barn you join a tarred farm road that runs past Lunga crags on the left, to reach the road junction at GR 954 834. Turn right here and walk a third of a mile to a left hand turning (GR 957 836). Turn left here and walk along the road, past a copse on your left, down to cross the Ray Burn at a culvert. Here a green footpath points to the north, signing the way to "Blaxter Cottages 4 miles". Turn right off the road to follow this path. You drop down a steep bank, across a tributary of the Ray Burn and then find yourself walking through a narrow bridge under the old railway line. This has now become a well used farm road. If you should want an escape route, you can turn right along this to take you eventually to the new hotel and filling station at Knowesgate.

The Reivers Way now goes uphill across a heathery patch of moor, to enter the mature pinewood. No path is discernible on the ground here, so use your compass. Make for a prominent break in the trees where the path enters the wood at GR 948 849. Two hundred yards after entering the wood, you find yourself on a good forest track, taking you down to the gate and bridge over the Lisles Burn. Turn right off the forest road here, through a hunting gate and head due north towards a wooden shed. From here the right of way is little used as it runs north across a heathery moor to the cottages at Wishaw. A certain amount of wading is necessary to cross the stream shortly before Wishaw. Head due north from Wishaw - the map a little out of date here - along the east side of Ray Fell plantation. From Scald Law you have a fine view of the Cheviots, lying several miles to the north. When you reach the gate at GR 940 891 turn left into the plantation and follow the route between the fence on your right and the close-packed trees on your left. This brings you to the entrance to the quarry on the main A 696 road. Cross the road here and

The attractive village of Rothbury (Photo: R.B.Evans)

Much of the walk lies within the Northumbrian National Park
(Photo: R.B.Evans)

The walk descends through the Rothbury Forest (Photo: R.B.Evans)
The way crosses Harthope Burn (Photo: R.B.Evans)

go through the gate. Keep the fence on your right as you descend to cross the stream, then head ever northwards over the western side of Middle Hill, down to cross Raylees Burn and up to the renovated cottage at Hillhead. From here the path to Elsdon is marked by stiles, though it is little used.

Arriving in Elsdon, you find yourself in a village that is almost more green than village, the houses forming a hollow square facing towards the Pele tower and St Cuthbert's church. For a time the Pele was the vicarage. Two centuries ago events at the Pele gave rise to the spot "Winter's Gibbet" at a lonely spot on the road from Elsdon to Cambo. One William Winter had robbed and murdered Margaret Crozier in the Pele tower one night in 1791. He was subsequently hanged at Newcastle and his body exhibited at the lonely spot which bears his name - the second last individual to be exhibited as a corpse. One may idly wonder if it was worthwhile to meet such a grisly end, thus to achieve immortality on an Ordnance Survey map. In the summer of 1992 the carved wooden head that was hung on the gibbet was removed, giving the local press an opportunity to make a few exaggerated headlines.

In 1938 an attempt was made to enclose some of the village green for use as a burial ground. This was resisted by the Northumberland and Newcastle Society and the green remains, a great expanse of common land in the centre of the village. During the nineteenth century, when alterations were taking place, a large number of skeletons were found, apparently buried in a communal grave. Since Elsdon never had the population which could produce so many deaths, say from plague, it seems likely that they were casualties from the Battle of Otterburn, fought on the night of 19th August 1388. The site can still be visited, half a mile north-west of the village. An information board on the main A696 road gives information about the battle fought between the

English and Scottish armies as the Scots retreated from Newcastle, laying the country waste as they did. Elsdon tower is now open to the public in the summer, by appointment only, although the grounds need no prior arrangement. Accommodation and refreshment can be found at the ancient Bird in Bush pub, on the far left corner of the hollow square.

CHAPTER 5
Elsdon to Rothbury
13 miles

There is neither pub nor shop between Elsdon and Rothbury, so you should buy some supplies from the wonderfully old-fashioned Post Office stores in Elsdon. Before you leave the village, visit the Motte and Bailey on the north east corner of the village, after the bridge. This is all that remains of a Norman castle built in the early 1100s by Robert de Umfraville, first Lord of Redesdale.

From Elsdon village green take the Rothbury road heading northwards. You cross the Elsdon Burn on a modern bridge and then turn right through a gate onto the unfenced road to Landshott and Eastnook. Continue on the road past the turning to Hudspeth, past Landshott farm and the entrance to Whiskershiel Farm. You go through another gate and enter the forest, walking up a steep incline. When you arrive at Whitlees Farm on your left, turn right into a narrow forest ride, taking you exactly to the junction of forest tracks at GR 963 926. A gap has been left through the trees, precisely following the route of the path taking you to Manside Cross. At approximately GR 977 923 you apparently come to a dead halt, trees blocking the way. This is where a forest road, not marked on the map, crosses the route from north to south. Push your way five yards through the trees and cross the road to pick up the continuation of the forest ride to Manside. The going is laborious, through deep heather and high tussocks of discampsia grass: this is not a regularly frequented path.

ELSDON TO ROTHBURY

ROTHBURY

WHITTON

B6341

RIVER COQUET

GT. TOSSON

ROTHBURY
FOREST

SIMONSIDE
HILLS

TOSSON
HILL

WEATHER
HEAD

SELBY'S
COVE

COQUET
CAIRN

BODDLE
MOSS

DARDEN
BURN

NEWBIGGIN

BURN

CHARTNERS

FALLOWLEES LOUGH

FALLOW
LEES

DARDEN
LOUGH

HARWOOD
FOREST

FALLOWLEES

BURN

RED
PATH

EAST
NOOK

WHITLEES

MANSIDE
CROSS

ELSDON

0 MILES
0 KM

N

A mile and a half after Whitlees you arrive, with some relief, at the clearing around the earthworks at Manside. The stump of the cross itself lies on the ground near the fence, so worn that it now resembles one of the phallic "lingam" stones found in ancient Hindu temples. From Manside the path runs exactly as the map shows, its route occasionally marked by scything the rough grass and heather. Near spot height 283 you would be as well to keep on the forest road, turning left to take the route signed to Chartners. At Redpath you find an old shepherd's cottage, now deep in the dismal woods. Keep heading north east (the footpath as marked on the map is disused), through the gate and after a mile of easy walking you reach the cottage at Fallowlees.

This is rather at variance with Wade's original version which had the walker spending almost the whole day away from rights of way. In fact my copy of the original has blank pages where the text should be for this section, but his sketch map is illuminating, showing as it does a route keeping to the west side of Harwood Forest, walking over King's Dod, by Dough Crag, the intriguingly named Gunner's Box and Tosson Hill. There is no right of way over this route and it should not be tried. Be warned that the temptingly direct path through the forest from Landshott Hill to Chartners simply does not exist on the ground. To try it would lead to an unpleasant day spent thrashing through close-packed conifers, the sort of stuff that is aptly called "fight" on an orienteering map. The dilemma is - what to do when a path exists on the map but is impassable through lack of use rather than deliberate blocking? Mapping and walking footpaths in this kind of terrain is trying indeed. A path that existed long before the land was reforested with Sitka plantation stands no chance of remaining open unless considerable effort is made. When such forests are planted, rides are left, not shown on the map. In a few years these become obvious corridors through the otherwise impenetrable growth of young conifers. Vehicles will tend to use these rides, followed by walkers - suddenly a track now exists where there was none before, bearing no relation to what is shown on the map.

Incidentally the bridle path that runs north west from Fallowlees to Hepple via Chartners is an attractive route, easy to walk and once out of the forest has very fine views.

However, to return to our route: from Fallowlees the path is marked clearly on the map as a bridle path heading north. As you near the top of the hill towards the end of the forest you pass a ruin on your left. Just after this the forest road turns sharply to the left: the path continues due north to a gate in the fence bounding the woods. Ahead lies the wonderful small gorge of Selby's cove, which is named on the map, but whose crags have escaped the cartographer's attention. At last the Reivers Way is on a path that is used to some degree. Follow it to the edge of the forest at the head of Selby's Cove and then directly to the summit ridge of Simonside.

In the vicinity of GR 027 985 pick up a path which takes you very steeply down the bracken-covered slope to the woods. Some felling has taken place. However the tracks in the forest are still as the map marks them. Follow the path from the summit to the junction at GR 031 989 (some of the trees have been cut down on the left here) and continue on the route marked by red triangles to the car park and picnic site at the bottom of the hill. Turn right on the road here and walk a quarter of a mile until the beginning of the wood on your left. Turn left here onto a signed bridle way to walk through the woods and turn left at the end to make your way past a small quarry now used as a rubbish tip (strangely enough, exactly on the National Park boundary). Just after the quarry turn right at the end of a narrow copse to take the farm track to Whitton Hillhead. The farm lane steadily improves as you approach Salter's Folly, marked "Tower" on the map. Whitton has a campsite and a hotel. For Rothbury itself, turn right at Whitton and then immediately left to pass through the car park of Whitton Farmhouse Hotel. The path now descends steeply, keeping well to the left of a row of council houses. You pass through a wicket gate at the end of a road. Walk down this to the road junction by the bridge.

The River Coquet's name is unusual in that it is of Anglo Saxon origin. In general in England, whilst place names are of post-Roman, Anglo-Saxon origin, rivers, in common with some other natural features, retained their Celtic names. The frequent recurrence of the name "Avon" is an example. The name "Coquet" is first found in the eleventh century in a document relating to Brinkburn, the now ruined priory downstream along the Coquet from Rothbury. The name is here rendered as "Cocwud" - which is exactly as one might imagine "cock-wood" or wood with birds. The valley derives its name from a forest. It seems likely that Coquetdale was so named and thus gave rise to the name of the river, rather than vice versa. However it got its name, the Coquet, along much of whose banks the next day will be spent is one of England's most delightful rivers.

The first mention of Rothbury dates from 1125 - the majority of English settlements have their first record of existence in the Domesday Book of William the Conqueror. In Northumberland the settlements are every bit as old as those further south, but the King's writ did not extend to these parts until well into the next century. As famous as the town itself now is the mansion of Cragside, built by the industrial and armaments magnate, Lord Armstrong, half an hour's walk from the town. It was designed in 1870 by Norman Shaw, who was chiefly an architect of Victorian Gothic churches. The house is a strange mishmash of styles popular at the time - similarly surreal buildings can be seen in the hill stations of India, such as Gorton Castle in Simla. The gardens are a romantic layout of azaleas, rhododendrons and artificial lakes. The town of Rothbury itself is simply one of the most delightful in England: particularly because it is relatively little visited and therefore has a much more attractive array of businesses than a comparable settlement in, say, the Cotswolds, overrun with antique shops and guest houses. No, in Rothbury you can buy a new pair of boots or a new jacket, sample several wonderfully old fashioned bakeries, browse in an ironmongers (and ponder the while the ignorant greed which has given rise to the vast DIY emporia of urban Britain). All this in a town which takes little more than five minutes to walk out of. Rothbury tempts the Reivers wayfarer to take a day off, once having arrived, by visiting the National Park Information Centre, followed by a visit to Cragside, a stroll to the church, a read of the paper.... Suddenly the day is gone, it is time to dive into a pub, order a bar meal (there is also a small Italian restaurant in the town) listen to the conversation, the day is over. Enjoy your time in Rothbury - towns like this are now few and far between in Britain.

CHAPTER 6

Rothbury to Uswayford
18 miles

This is a day's walk that takes you from the leafy vale of the Coquet, northwards, high into the Cheviot Hills: it is the most challenging day yet on the Reivers Way. If you do not have a tent, make sure of your night's accommodation with a telephone call to Uswayford Farm before attempting Clennell Street. This lonely farm is much in demand as lodging by walkers along the dismal trudge of the Pennine Way.

From the centre of Rothbury, take the B6341 road towards Elsdon. At the end of the green bank in the village, fork right up a side road at St Agnes Roman Catholic church, following a sign for Pondicherry. Follow this road for just over half a mile, past a number of detached properties sited to gain the best possible views of the Simonside hills across the valley. The road becomes a rough track with grass up the middle, then returns to tarmac as you go up the hill. You turn right onto a footpath into a copse of scattered oak and rowan where the now private road swings to the left. The path goes straight to the top of the hill above the old fort (marked spot height 185 on the map). Ahead the rounded outlines of Cold Law and Harden Hill and the higher Cheviot peaks behind beckon. Walk down the hill across the fields to cross over the overgrown old farm track at a stile and keep heading down the hill, making for a stile in the hedge at a prominent ash tree to arrive at the road junction at GR 033 026. Walk up the

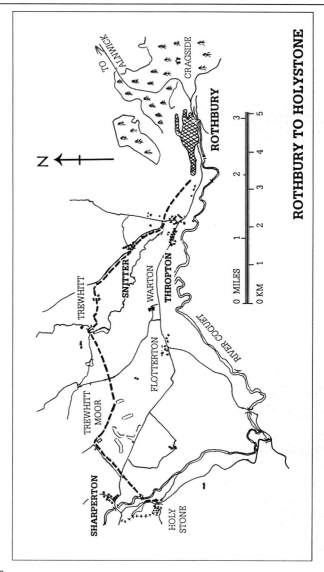

ROTHBURY TO HOLYSTONE

public road leading to Netherton and the hamlet of Snitter.

Continue up the Netherton road for a mile and a half and turn left down the access road to Low Trewhitt and Snitter Windyside. Follow this tarred farm lane for three quarters of a mile, across the bridge over the Netherton Burn which appears shortly after a sharp right hand bend. Turn left immediately over the bridge with its lonely post box to cross the Foxton Burn at a constructed ford and footbridge and go up the hill with a new barn on your left. Follow this good farm track, through several double gates to meet the road on Trewhitt Moor (GR 990 040). Now follow the footpath due west, gently uphill to meet the right hand end of a narrow copse of tall Scots Pine. Walk through a gate in the wall here. The path now swings to the right, down to cross the Trewhitt Burn at a gate by the corner of a stone wall, then diagonally up the hill to reach the farm at Sharperton Edge. Turn left along the road here and walk down, past Charity Hall Farm on your left, to the T-junction marked on the map with spot height 168. Cross the Sharperton road and take the bridle path down to cross the Coquet at a fine footbridge. Turn left along the road for a quarter of a mile to the village of Holystone. The hamlet of Sharperton has no pub, but bed and breakfast is available at Bounty Cottage (see Appendix).

You should time your arrival at Holystone to coincide with the opening hours of the Salmon Inn. This is in fact quite a moveable feast - many years ago I walked into the Salmon at midnight to find it in full swing and serving. It is certainly one of the most delightful pubs in the county.

Leave the pub and take the footpath signed on the right to Lady's Well, a wonderfully clear pool surrounded by trees. Continue northwards past this, downhill over several stiles to join the Sharperton-Harbottle road opposite the row of cottages at Wood Hall. Turn left here on the road. Be warned that the bridle-way shown crossing the Coquet at GR 953 041

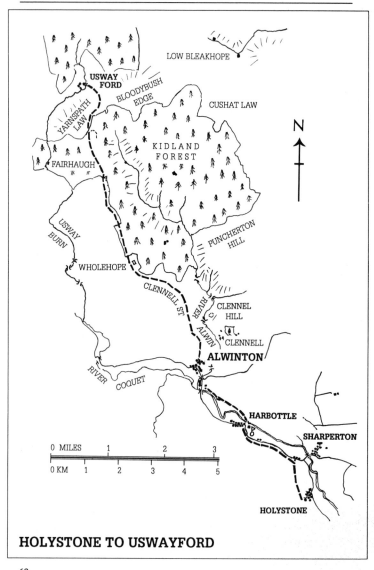

HOLYSTONE TO USWAYFORD

does not exist on the ground. It is a pity, because the track heading north west to The Peels, on the north side of the Coquet, is pleasant indeed. Instead, walk into Harbottle on the road.

The first mention of the village is from around 1220, as "Hyrbotle". The first element is variously claimed to be "hireling", or, more dramatically "Here", as expressed in the Anglo-Saxon chronicle, a host or army. There is evidence of fortification having been on the site of the present castle since around or before the time of the Norman conquest. It is said that everyone once in his or her life is famous, if only for a short time. So it is with settlements, too. The study of the history of many a village will generally reveal a short time when the great affairs of the world were its concern. Harbottle's "hour upon the stage" occurred in the following way. When Henry VII ascended the throne following the Battle of Bosworth in 1485, he was determined to bring in a period of peace following the Wars of the Roses that had brought him to the throne. He married Elizabeth of York, to end forever the York-Lancaster feud. His daughter Margaret, sister of the future Henry VIII, he married to James IV of Scotland, precipitating eventually the accession of a Stuart to the throne when Henry VIII's daughter Elizabeth died childless. In 1515 Margaret gave birth in Harbottle Castle to the mother of Lord Darnley, the father of James VI of Scotland and I of England. Sadly that castle building is no more. It is possible to stay in Harbottle, at Waterloo House. There is also the fine Star Inn, on the right hand side just after the Reivers Way takes you off the road through the village.

As you walk into the village, turn right as though you were going to approach the castle. (This is not the same castle as mentioned above - the ruins of this can be seen at the western end of the village, beyond the pub.) Immediately before the castle, turn left onto a footbridge and cross the

Coquet. Just over the bridge turn left to take the track to Low Alwinton, overlooking the confluence of the rivers Coquet and Alwin - the "white river". Turn right on the road here and walk into Alwinton. If you have not been too long delayed in the Salmon or the Star, you should be in time to fortify yourself at the Rose and Thistle before tackling the rigours of Clennell Street. The name Rose and Thistle commemorates its location as the last pub in England before the border. Beyond Alwinton, the road along the bottom of Coquetdale is a dead end. Nevertheless it runs for many miles, serving the isolated farms. On the second Saturday in October Alwinton is the scene of a great agricultural show, a gathering of the sheep-rearing clans from round about.

From the Rose and Thistle, retrace your steps to cross the Hosedon Burn. Turn left along the farm road heading north - a wooden signpost points the way. As you leave Alwinton on a farm track of grey rubble you are walking along Clennell Street. This is one ancient route in the area that is not Roman in origin, but an old drovers' road. It is referred to in mediaeval charters as *"magnum viam de Yarnspath"*. If you walked its whole length from Alwinton, it would take you over the border, to the village of Cocklawfoot. The first settlement it reaches, however, has the same name as the route itself - Clennellstreet. This is a former hamlet, now just a cottage. Below you to your right is the collection of houses at Clennel, including a Pele dating from 1365. The path is now a well-defined grassy track running northwards up the spur between the valleys of the Alwinton Burn and the River Alwin. Ahead lie the massed conifers of Kidland Forest, largely avoided by your path. You keep the forest on your right as you pass Wholehope (pronounced "Woolup"), now ruined, but formerly a youth hostel.

Immediately after Wholehope the path drops into a gully and you see a wooden gate in front of you. Go through this, now on a driveable forest road, and keep left at the junction immediately inside the forest. As I strolled along this forest road, with a view of nothing but close-packed conifers, I pondered the following question. If an individual plants a forest he naturally wants to see profit in his own lifetime - the planting of relatively quick growing Sitka for pulp is understandable. The government, surely, does not have to reap profit within the span of a human life. We read of the damage caused by cropping unsustainable tropical hardwoods. When the north transept of York Minster had to be reroofed following the fire started by lightning, scarcely a single oak tree of sufficient size could be found in Britain. Hardwoods used in furniture and building are certainly more valuable per cubic metre than pulp on which to print the newspapers. Dense arboreal monoculture does not enhance the landscape. Why then does not the government's Forestry Commission, where altitude permits, plant native hardwoods much in demand as valuable timber, such as oak or beech?

Anyway, after just over half a mile you exit from the plantation, crossing Saughy Hill. You have very fine views of the Cheviot itself as you walk on to Nettlehope Hill. As you descend on the north side of Nettlehope the track divides at a fine fork, just as the map shows. Keep right here, as Clennell Street bends away and down to the left. You now have just over half a mile of walking in the woods before you reach what the map marks as the end of the forest road at GR 889 129. In fact the road does not end here, but twists around the head of the valley of the East Burn and heads back into the plantation. Turn left off the road here, on a little-used path and leave the confines of Kidland Forest behind at a stile. As you look to your right, along the edge of the woods you will see the rounded summit of Bloodybush Edge. The right of way takes you across the peat and heather to the broad col between Bloodybush Edge and Yarnspath Law. From here you descend steeply to Uswayford Farm. This, one of the remotest farms in England, provides bed and breakfast (see Appendix). Be sure to telephone well in advance, for the accommodation here is much in demand by walkers along the Pennine Way. Bear in mind that, strictly speaking, it is illegal to camp wild in the forest through which you have just walked.

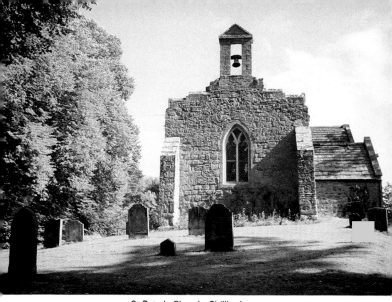

St Peter's Church, Chillingham

A trip to the Farne Islands is recommended to see the prolific birds and seals, as well as the site of Grace Darling's epic rescue. (Photo: R.B.Evans)

Low Newton is an attractive hamlet by the sea. (Photo: R.B.Evans)
Looking northwards to Dunstanburgh Castle

CHAPTER 7
Uswayford to Wooler
18 miles

Wade's original route over the Cheviot, written before anyone could foresee the enormously damaging impact of thousands of walkers each year on the Pennine Way, ran from Uswayford to join Salters Road and then to the sheep fence which marks the border at GR 872 161. From here it followed the Pennine Way and border fence for three miles to a stile and a walkers' signpost at a sharp left hand bend in the fence at GR 896 194. Continuing north and east, it ran to the top of Cairn Hill, then the Cheviot. From the Cheviot it headed north-east, marked on the map by a black pecked line, over Scald Hill, then descended to the broad saddle south of Broadhope Hill. Here on the map is a T-junction of paths, with a choice of routes to Broadstruther, one via the Lambden Valley to the west, the other via the Hawsen valley to the east. Wade, with his trademark disregard for rights of way, plotted a route directly over Broadhope Hill to Broadstruther.

During the seventies this was a pleasant and wild route. Now, however, it has seen some of the worst erosion by walkers along this stretch of Britain's most famous long distance path. The repeated passage of feet has removed the ground cover of cotton grass, tussocks and heather. Thus laid bare, the peat turns to spongey mud. Walkers naturally avoid this, and keep to a route on either side, thus perpetually widening the belt of erosion. Around Butt Roads, pallets and even stone paving slabs have been laid on the denuded peat - a dismal perversion of what hillwalking should be. At the

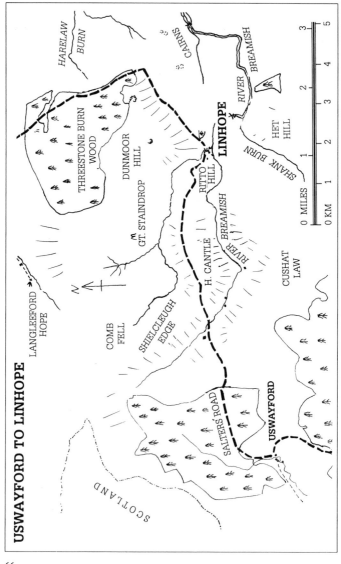

USWAYFORD TO LINHOPE

time of writing more slabs were to be airlifted in. To hark back to the introduction, walkers here most certainly have killed what they love. This stretch of the Pennine Way is an eloquent condemnation of the whole concept of long distance footpaths. Though the walking may be lamentable, the views to the north into Scotland are very fine. Beyond Cheviot Summit (itself one large peat bog) there is less erosion but still large amounts of eternally wet peat to be negotiated.

Happily, there is an alternative to the endless peat of the Pennine Way and the Cheviot and this should be followed for two reasons - it is a far more pleasant and interesting walk and it avoids further damaging the environment. Leave Uswayford along the eastern side of the Usway Burn, walking due north. After a third of a mile you reach the confluence with the Clay Burn and the waterfall. Jump across the Clay Burn here, a tiny gorge to your right, and follow its western bank due north and then north west. Just over half a mile after the waterfall you meet the bridle path of Salter's Road as it heads due east up to the col between Lint Lands and Bloodybush Edge. A wooden signpost marks the junction at GR 890 155. Salter's Road is originally a prehistoric route, its exact origins unknown. In more recent times it was used by traders taking salt from the mouth of the Tyne into Scotland, hence its name. In Elsdon churchyard, passed on the previous day's walk, is the tomb of one Thomas Wilson "officer for the duty of salt", who died in 1778. It was at this time that the Salters' Roads earned their name. It would in itself make a fine walk, connecting Alnham (GR 99 10) to Kirk Yetholm, across the border. From the map it looks as though there is half an hour's repeat of Kidlandlee Forest: in fact Salter's road lies along a wide grassy strip, with fine views, a happy relief from the claustrophobia of the usual forest tracks.

Follow Salter's Road as it leaves the woods and descends over the knoll of Nagshead Knowe by a grey barn, to the confluence of the River Breamish with the Ainsey Burn. The head of the Breamish valley is a beautiful hollow in the bracken-covered hills. The following day we meet the River Breamish again, having changed its name to the Till. You cross a footbridge and come to an old railway wagon used as a sheep shed, just before a small copse not marked on the map. From this shed the path runs up the steep slope, through a narrow gate in a wall to reach the grouse moors around the summit of High Cantle. There is little sign of this route ever being walked, so you will have to use your compass and read the contours. From High Cantle, the path runs east, through deep heather, following a broad spur between the valleys of the Linhope Burn and the River Breamish. You go through a gate in a fence and leave the grouse moor behind you and head along a fence over the bare moor and tussocks.

Across the valley of the Coldlaw Burn is the prominent knoll of Great Staindrop, standing just before Hedgehope Hill. In fact Hedgehope Hill itself is a better viewpoint and altogether a better hill to climb than Cheviot itself. There is little marked in the way of a path until you meet a track running away to the left as you cross a gentle saddle before Ritto Hill. Join this track as it becomes a road, running past the trees. Linhope Spout, a fine waterfall, makes a worthwhile diversion, just to the north of the woods. Follow the road down, past the farmhouse on the left and over the bridge. Leave Linhope along the gated road to Hartside. Immediately after the bridge a new gravel track turns off the road to the left, not marked on the map. At the end of the trees you open a gate to walk on a good bridleway across the springy close-cropped turf. This is used as a farm lane, not marked on the map, which swings away to the right. The path, seldom used, now takes you across the bottom of the long straight slope of Dunmoor Hill. This is wonderful terrain, the slopes above

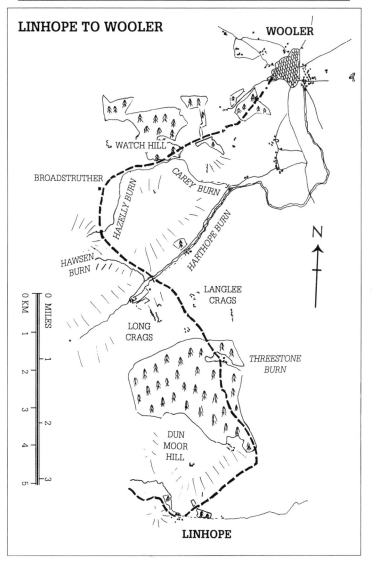

LINHOPE TO WOOLER

WOOLER

WATCH HILL

BROADSTRUTHER

CAREY BURN

HAZELLY BURN

HARTHOPE BURN

HAWSEN BURN

N

LANGLEE CRAGS

LONG CRAGS

THREESTONE BURN

0 MILES
0 KM

DUN MOOR HILL

LINHOPE

The upper Breamish valley

you on the left a tangle of bare rocks and bracken. To your right, the landscape is scattered with ancient earthworks and settlements. Most of the path lies through bracken. You pass a black sheep shed near an unmarked path junction.

Just past the "Village Earthworks" featured on the map, barely discernible on the ground, a footpath takes you off the to the left, due north to the corner of Threestoneburn Wood. Thankfully the edge of the wood is just as the map marks. In fact the trees are hidden from view by the lie of the land until just before you reach them. At the corner of the plantation a gate leads you through the fence. Head north west along the gap between the fence and the trees, a vestigial path just discernible on the ground. After a third of a mile you come to a gate in the fence to your right (GR 983 185). Turn left here and you find yourself, just as the map shows, at the end of a forest road, where you turn right.

Follow this track due north as it crosses two barely discernible trickles in the woods in quick succession. These are the Harelaw Burn and its tributary. You arrive at the track junction, exactly as the map marks at GR 975 198: turn left here and after fifty yards turn to the right - a break in the trees has been made for the path. A path through the clearing, marked by a post, leads you down the hill and on to the next map to bring you to Threestoneburn House. This former shooting lodge is now an elegant weekend retreat. At the house there are two paths heading off to the east and north east. The one that is not marked on the map is a permissive path rather than a statutory right of way, negotiated by the National Park authorities. The two are marked in the same way on the ground. You turn left as you reach Threestoneburn House and cross the stream on a new wooden footbridge leading into the garden. Bear left, following the north bank of the stream, walking back into the trees at a gate marked with a yellow arrow. From the edge of the forest the path leads north west, barely marked on the ground over the ridge between Langlee Crags and Housey Crags. As you begin to descend into the Harthope Valley the path becomes clearer. As marked on the map the path turns sharply towards the right at GR 957 225. In fact a permissive path heads straight down to cross the river at a good footbridge at GR 955 225.

Less than half a mile up the valley is Langleeford Farm where Sir Walter Scott stayed in 1791. He described the farm as having "one of the wildest and most romantic situations". He also wrote that "so much simplicity resides among these hills that a pen, which could write at least, was not to be found about the house, though belonging to a considerable farmer, till I shot the crow with whose quill I wrote this epistle." Walk up to the road here and a little to the right a path turns off to the left to take you along the side of the valley of Hawsen Burn. After half a mile the path forks - take the right hand fork (a bridleway) up to the col and due north to Broadstruther. After you leave the Hawsen Valley you reach

Looking across Harthope Burn to Langlee Crags and Long Crags.
Photo: B.Evans

"postman's gate" in the fence, where the postman, in the days when he went on foot, left the letters. The path heads north, crosses the Hazelly Burn and leads up to the ruin at Broadstruther.

From Broadstruther a bridle path takes you straight to the confluence of the Hazelly Burn and Common Burn, and then along Hell's Path into the pinewoods on the flanks of Watch Hill. You exit from the woods by a cairn, from where the path takes you between two plantations to the farm at Wooler Common. Keep the farm buildings on your right, and head due west to a fork in the bridleways. Ignore the turning to the left on to the road and head up the hill into the pine wood cloaking the northern side of Earle Whin hill. This is a well trodden path, supplied with seats for the weary population of Wooler and it leads you out on to an expanse of gorse and turf, in days gone by a golf course. Walk down the hill to the end of the drive to The Waud House. Turn right on the public road to walk down Common Road into the fine little market town of Wooler. You are now back on the original Reivers Way.

Wooler marks the transition of the Reivers Way from the Cheviot Hills to the arable country stretching away to what the poet Swinburn calls the "lordly strand" of Northumberland's coast. From the solid architecture of the town centre you could almost be in Scotland already. "Wulloure" is first mentioned in 1187 in Pipe Rolls. The name appears to mean "stream bank" - "well" being "stream" and "ofer" (cf modern German "Ufer") meaning bank. The baronry was held by one Robert de Muschampe, in return for which he was bound to provide four knights for royal service. The early Motte and Bailey was already derelict by the thirteenth century but was rebuilt in the 1500s. A few remains can be seen overlooking Church Street. Now there is a wide choice of hotel and bed and breakfast accommodation.

The main street at Wooler. Photo: B.Evans

CHAPTER 8
Wooler to Bamburgh
18 miles

Leave the market place in the centre of Wooler along down The Peth, over the bridge towards Morpeth. Immediately over the bridge is a left hand turning, along Brewery Road, taking you towards Glendale school and the dish-shaped television transmitters on Weetwood Moor in front of you. After half a mile the road turns sharply to the right as you go up hill beneath some trees. At this right hand bend, the original Reivers Way leads largely across the arable land to Belford. Here you must decide whether or not you are going to make the very worthwhile diversion to Chillingham, lying three miles to the south east. If you do, your route lies along the road which rapidly deteriorates to a green track, heading south east to West Lilburn Hall, an unusual wooden house at GR 033 258, through Newtown and over the bridge over the River Till. Ahead of you rises a fine ridge behind Chillingham.

The castle itself is in a superb setting, with the towering heights of Ros Castle, an old Celtic hill-top fort behind it. Chillingham is famous for its herd of wild white cattle. A distinction should be made between wild and merely feral, which is stock descended from domestic beasts now living wild. The Chillingham cattle are truly wild and unique in Britain, roaming in a park which was walled in in 1220, thus isolating the herd from the outbreaks of foot and mouth disease which periodically decimated domestic cattle. They are a strain of the original European wild ox and retain all the characteristics of wild animals - it is not permitted to wander

WOOLER TO TWIZEL OR BELFORD

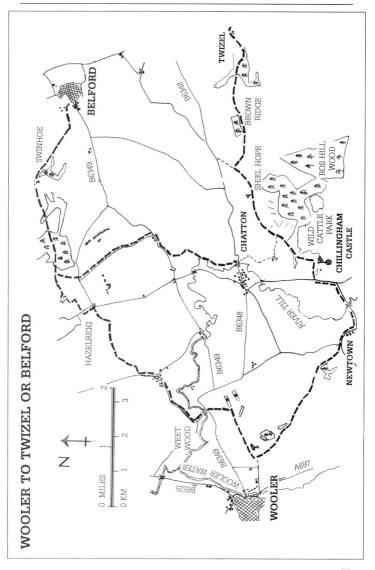

Chillingham Castle

into their park at will, for obvious safety reasons. However permission can be obtained from the park keeper. In what seems now a bizarre and ghoulish ritual, the then Prince of Wales (later Edward VII) with Alexandra of Denmark, the Princess of Wales, visited Chillingham in 1872 and was invited to shoot the dominant male in the herd, the "king bull". As was the custom of the time, his photograph was taken with his grisly trophy. The cattle are now in the care of the Chillingham Wild Cattle Association and can be seen with the park warden every day except Tuesdays - the castle can be visited every afternoon except Tuesdays, from 1.30 onwards. The Post Office marked on the map has now closed. Saint Peter's church in Chillingham, dating from the twelfth century is well worth a visit, with its fine monument to a former incumbent of Chillingham, Sir Ralph Grey and his wife.

If you really want to make a day of it, you should walk up to Ros Castle (1035ft), the site of a prehistoric hill fort where the National Trust and Forestry Commission have built a viewing platform. In clear weather you can see seven castles

Ornamental Park cattle at Chillingham - not the Wild White cattle
Photo: B.Evans

- Warkworth, lying further south than the end of the Reivers Way, Alnwick, Ford, Chillingham, Bamburgh, Lindisfarne and Dunstanburgh. The shortest way to return to the Reivers Way from Chillingham is to walk northwards along the road to the village of Chatton: a few yards after the bridge just before the village, turn right across a sports ground (a caravan serving as pavilion) to walk across the fields and into the churchyard. What does make a visit to Chatton worthwhile is the Percy Arms. This is a smart hotel which welcomes walkers, despite apparently catering largely for middle aged Rover-driving consumers of bar meals. There is also a village shop and an ancient Pele tower incorporated into the old vicarage.

Leave Chatton on the main B6348 road due east towards Seahouses and cross back over the river. At the end of the bridge, turn left, down a set of steps, to follow the footpath northwards to meet the farm lane just before crossing the

Lyham Burn at a ford and footbridge. Turn left on this track, and walk a third of a mile along it to meet the B6349 road from Wooler to Belford where you turn right. Immediately after the farm at Old Lyham with its prominent roof of old red tiles, turn left and follow the road a mile and a half to the north to rejoin the Reivers Way at Hazelrigg.

You may well wish to shorten the day's walk by heading directly to Waren Mill, avoiding Belford. Keep along the tarred lane that swings to the left under the trees by the church in Chillingham. It turns to a track - keep left where the track forks. This route was constructed for the visit of the Prince of Wales in 1872 and is known as "The Drive". Follow this good track past Sheilhope (GR 082 281). Half a mile after the farm you reach the end of a wood on your left. Turn right here through a metal farm gate, head for a stone sheep fold and follow the path to the conifer plantation to the left of the empty farm at Brownridge (GR 100 284). Keep the farm on your right and follow the southern edge of the wood past a prefabricated building down to Cocklaw Dean woods. You turn left onto a tarred road, and walk down to cross the Waren Burn at a footbridge and ford and through Twizel. Turn right immediately after the farm at a footpath sign and walk under the main A1 on a path, emerging into the grounds of a house. You leave Warenford on the road to Lucker, turn right after thirty yards and follow the path along the Waren Burn to the Apple Inn. The path beyond Lucker, passing under the main line tends to be overgrown and flooded - you may prefer to take the road to Bradford, then the path passing to the right of a large new barn, along the edge of the field, crossing the tributary of the Waren Burn at a rickety footbridge (GR 151 329), to Spindlestone Farm, then down the road to Waren Mill. The Chillingham diversion, returning via Chatton and Hazelrigg adds four miles to the day's walk, returning via Warenford and Lucker adds just one mile.

The alignment of the original path, avoiding Chillingham, is as follows: a footpath takes you diagonally up the steep slope to cross the northern edge of Weetwood Moor. Look north west from the top of the hill and a mile away you see the point where the Till joins Wooler Water. After a few more meandering miles it is joined by the River Glen, giving rise to the name Glendale. On the far side of Glendale, within sight of Weetwood Moor, is the site of the battle of Bosworth Field, a battle about which much more is popularly known than the war of which it was but a part. In 1513 the English King Henry VIII was with the English army in France. The Scottish invasion in support of the Auld Alliance can almost be seen as a diversion. The English army that opposed it was hastily assembled from the northern shires under the Earl of Surrey. Battle was joined at 4.00 on the afternoon of Friday 9th September and by nightfall the Scottish King, James IV, was dead as were scores of Scottish nobility and up to 10,000 Scotsmen. Not until 1st July 1916 did one battle affect so many families. Nowadays a simple cross marks the spot where the Scottish king is supposed to have fallen. It reads "To the Brave of both Nations". At the top of Weetwood Moor the path forks: take the left hand fork, past spot height 148 marked on the map. Away to the left Doddington Moor rises beyond the alluvial valley floor where the Wooler Water meets the River Till. Looking back towards Wooler from Weetwood Moor the Cheviot summits rise behind the town. Furthest right of these is Yeavering Bell, mentioned by Bede as "Ad Gefrin", the hilltop capital of Northumbria in the time of the Christian King Edwin. Aerial surveys and excavations have confirmed settlement on the spot.

As you descend on the eastern side of Weetwood Moor, you reach the end of a rectangular plantation and a path junction at GR 020 287. Turn left here and walk northwards, down the hill to the fine stone arch of Weetwood Bridge.

Follow the road up the hill and north east to the farms and West and East Horton. Here you turn left on the road signed to Lowick. After 300 yards you turn right along a farm lane, taking you just south of the summit of Town Law. The path takes you north east, crossing the Hetton Burn, rejoining the road at the old school building at GR 049 327. Turn left along the road here, and after a quarter of a mile, turn right along the twisting tarred drive to North Hazelrigg. At North Hazelrigg the road passes in front of a row of pinkish farm cottages. Turn right beneath an old green water tower and take note of the new gravel farm road, not marked on the map, leading away to the north east. Avoid this by turning right through a gate, with a hedge on your left and walk along the back of the cottages. This path is not waymarked on the ground but can be followed. At the end of the plantation on your right, turn left and make for a gate at the top of the ploughed field. Turn right on the farm track leading from Holburn Grange Farm, then follow the edge of the ploughed field to enter the woods by a stile at GR 059 339. Now pick up the green arrows leading you in a complex zig-zag, now on woodland rides, now ducking through the trees to bring you after rather a long half mile to the track junction at GR 070 342.

Just to the north is Cuthbert's Cave, at a lonely spot looking out to sea from the ridge between Cockenheugh and Greensheen Hill. This is well worth a few minutes' diversion. The route now runs along a stony farm track with the first close, exhilarating views of the sea, north east to Swinhoe Farm. Turn right at the farm, where a sign points the way to Belford. Initially you are on a farm lane, which quickly becomes a footpath. Head between a crag and the end of the long copse to follow its eastern edge along a fine ridge. From here onwards the path is well waymarked across the flat fields, eventually bringing you along a low parapet to a bridge on the drive to West Hall and so into Belford. Belford

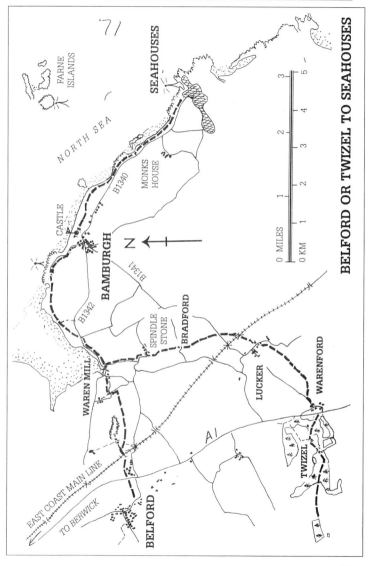

BELFORD OR TWIZEL TO SEAHOUSES

81

carries the air of a village that has never really come to terms with being bypassed by the Great North Road, having had it pass through the centre for centuries. Its principal grocer is in a kind of warehouse on the right as you come into the village. The Blue Bell is a pleasant pub, looking out onto the recently remodelled centre of the village.

From Belford, take the old Great North Road southwards, past the garage on the right. Shortly after this you see a golf driving range on the left hand side, and a footpath sign indicating the route to Waren Mill and some tall grain siloes ahead. Follow this between a wire mesh fence and the Belford Burn. As the little stream curves away to the left, the path keeps straight ahead under a line of trees to a stile and the main A1, here just single carriageway where the mighty lorries thunder along on their way to Scotland, trailing great banners of spray in the wet. Cross over the road, through another stile and keep the complex of siloes to your right. Now keep straight ahead with a fence on your right: as this turns to the right, towards the road, keep straight ahead to a stile and a warning sign on the railway. On your right is the old Belford station, now used as a road freight depot. This is the east coast main line, carrying the InterCity 225 trains at enormous speed - take great care here. In fact all crossings on the line around here are at level crossings. Once over the main railway line the path is less well defined. Keep straight ahead to a stile at the left hand end of a hedge along the now disused quarry line. Cross over this line and make for the corner of the potholed road to the quarry, straight ahead.

Walk along the road and keep straight ahead where the road turns left. From here on the path is not well waymarked; it takes you through a small gate and then runs along a wall on the right. When you reach the road at GR 143 341 a footpath sign points the way back to Belford Station. Turn left along the road into a dip with a small copse on the right. You are now in a small avenue of horse chestnuts. Turn right at a footpath sign pointing through a gate and follow the path along the edge of a wood, through a thick hedge and so into Waren Mill, pronounced "Wairen Mill". Across the road is the entrance to the camp and caravan site; there is a bar here which serves meals in the summer season. Turn left along the road, then right at the junction to cross the Waren Burn by the old mill. Formerly Waren Mill was sea port for Bamburgh, which received a charter from Henry II. Its port facilities declined earlier this century and now it wears a ghostly aspect - the archetypal silted up, deserted small seaport. Follow the Bamburgh road with its fine views, across Budle Bay where the tide ebbs to reveal an expanse of shining sands, northwards to the castle perched on the rock on Holy Island.

Just after the lane leading down to Kiln point, turn left along a footpath towards the shore. You reach the drive serving Heather Cottages; turn left along this for a few yards,

The Stag Rock north of Bamburgh. Photo: B.Evans

Bamburgh Castle. Photo: G.Cade

and then right along a bridle path, just inland of Budle Point, along the seaward side of the golf course. Half a mile after Heather Cottages you reach a stile by the club house and walk along the street called the Wyndings, past Harkness rocks on your left, into the village of Bamburgh, the wall of the castle towering over you.

Bamburgh is possibly the most dramatic of the famous castles that embellish the coast of Northumberland. It is unusual in that it is still inhabited. The first fortification here was built in 547 by King Ida the Flamebearer of Northumbria (a much larger entity than present-day Northumberland). For a while this fort, known as Dinguard, was the capital of the kingdom of Northumbria. Ida's grandson King Ethelfrith gave Dinguard to his wife, named Bebba, and the castle thereby acquired her name, later shortened to Bamburgh. Aidan, invited by King (later canonised) Oswald of Northumbria from Iona to convert his subjects, died at

Bamburgh, and his body was rowed to Holy Island to be buried. The castle lay desolate following the Viking attacks (the first of these being within sight, at Lindisfarne in 793), then passed into royal hands following the Norman conquest. Every castle likes to have a romantic episode in its history: Bamburgh's example was its surrender to William Rufus, son of William the Conqueror, by Matilda, Countess of Northumberland. She was blackmailed by the king who threatened to put out the eyes of her husband Robert. Margaret of Anjou, queen to Henry VI, held court here during the Wars of the Roses. From Bamburgh she rode out to do battle at Hexham in 1464, the site of which was passed near Corbridge, on the first day of the walk. In the eighteenth century the castle was the property of Lord Crewe, Bishop of Durham, who restored it; the ancient hotel at the bottom of the village commemorates him, as does the hotel in the wonderful village of Blanchland, three miles from the first day's walk. Of the structure still standing, the keep is Norman. A great deal of the present building is less than a century old, dating from extensive restoration made by Lord Armstrong (encountered at Cragside outside Rothbury a few days before) in 1894. The Castle is open to the public from Easter to the end of October, and now houses the Armstrong Museum of industrial heritage. Also in the village is the museum commemorating Grace Darling, the lighthouse keeper's daughter who became a heroine in 1838 for her involvement in the rescue of those aboard the Forfarshire, a steamer.

CHAPTER 9
Bamburgh to Alnmouth station
19 miles

Before starting the day's walk, it is a good idea to telephone ahead to Alnmouth station to ascertain the time of the train to make for in the afternoon, at the end of this final day's walk.

From Bamburgh the B1340 road runs along the coast: the walker along the Reivers Way can escape the traffic by walking along the sandy shore, keeping to the landward side of the rocky outcrops of Islestone, Greenhill Rocks, Monk's House Rocks and along St Aidan's dunes to the village of Seahouses itself. Sadly, the working seaport seems to be in danger of being swamped by amusement arcades and take-away food shops. Nowadays perhaps the only attraction to Seahouses is the possibility, between May and September, of taking the boat out to the Farne Islands. The Farnes are inhabited only by the warden of the wildlife sanctuary and the lighthouse keepers. The islands are one of Britain's most important sites for wildlife - namely grey seals and seabirds. Guillemots, fulmars, razorbills and a number of other species nest cheek by jowl on the ledges and the islands' rabbit population (introduced by the monks) provide homes for nesting puffins. The herd of grey seals, the only one on Britain's east coast, haul out to raise their pups in the autumn. Landing is not permitted between 15th May and 15th July to prevent disturbance to the islands' population of breeding seabirds.

Grey seals on the Farne Islands. Photo: G.Cade

Keep to the sea front in Seahouses, around the headland past Braidcarr Point and North Point, crossing the Annstead Burn on the road bridge, then returning to the beach. Alternatively you can if you wish avoid the coast road to Beadnell by taking the footpath from North Sunderland heading south east. You cross the Swinehoe Burn and the farm lane from Annstead Farm at a copse. In Beadnell take the road down to the harbour, pausing should you wish at the Craster Arms. You leave Beadnell along the beach, avoiding the route marked on the map through the serried ranks of "mobile homes". You head inland for 400 yards to cross the Brunton Burn on a good footbridge. The well used path takes you across Tughall Dunes and over the Brunton Burn on a good footbridge with the runway marker lights of Brunton airfield glowing away to your right. You continue southwards through the National Trust reserve of Newton Links to reach the car park. Turn right for ten yards up the

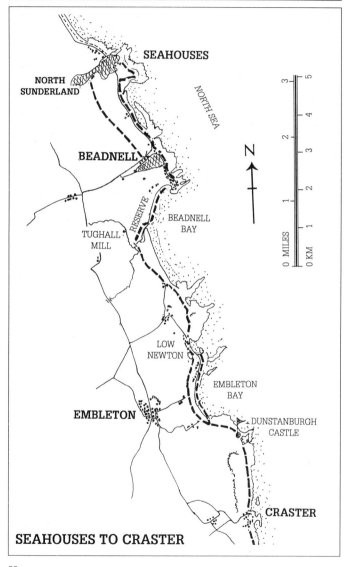

SEAHOUSES TO CRASTER

road here before continuing along the seaward edge of the fields to Football Hole, over a road and into Low Newton by the Sea.

It would be a shame to continue further without stopping at the Ship Inn. Low Newton, when it is not swamped by car-borne visitors on a summer holiday weekend, is an enchanting hamlet overlooking a small bay where the cobles bob on the tide. Cobles are the local fishing boats, reputedly developed from Viking craft, to which they bear some resemblance. They are deep in the bow so as to breast the rough seas of the coast and often have their propellers protected by strakes in the flat stern to permit beaching. The local crab and salmon served in the village are delicious. From the pub double round the back of the row of cottages to your left and head along a gravel path back into the dunes among a collection of seaside shacks. You walk through the dunes to find yourself on the the great sweep of sand around Embleton Bay, with the ruins of Dunstanburgh Castle ahead. Here the foreshore can be walked at all stages of the tide, the Embleton Burn proving no obstacle. As you approach the rocks on the south side of the Bay, walk up the bank to follow the path along the edge of the golf course past a Second World War pill box and around the landward side of Dunstanburgh Castle. There are few castles as dramatic as this not reached by car; happily Dunstanburgh is still approached as it always has been, by muscle power. The castle was built in 1314 and was so severely damaged by cannon in the Wars of the Roses that it was abandoned. It is thus a rare example of a fourteenth century castle that has escaped alteration or restoration. Formerly there was a small harbour here, now silted up and grassed over.

The sandy bays of Beadnell, Budle and Embleton are now behind and the path lies along a rocky shore where fields grazed by frisky steers slope down to the lichen-covered slabs, haunt of eider and shelduck. As you walk south towards the houses at Craster clustering on the shore, take time to turn and look back to Dunstanburgh. You are nearing the end of one the finest stretches of Britain's coastline.

Whilst the scenery is unmatchable, the food is equally hard to beat. If you are walking the route in late summer, you should already have sampled the melt-in-the-mouth crab and salmon at Newton or Embleton. Craster most certainly should not be walked through without sampling the kippers. Even if you think you don't like kippers, try one at the restaurant attached to Robson's smokehouse. A kipper here bears as much relation to the miserable offering in most supermarkets, full of artificial dyes and E numbers, as does a quarter pounder in Macdonald's to a rare fillet steak. The fish itself appears wrinkled - when cut it still retains the natural colour. The flavour is simply exquisite - it bears comparison with Scottish smoked salmon. At the time of writing it seems that EC directives may dictate the closure of the entire establishment, meaning that Craster kippers - the two words are as closely bonded as "Worcester" and "sauce" - will be a thing of the past. Under new regulations the smokehouse will have to be refurbished: it is up for sale and one can only hope that a buyer will be found prepared to make the necessary investment to meet new regulations and continue smoking Craster kippers over oak chips in the time-honoured way. As well as the restaurant in Craster, there is a fine pub over the road.

With the feet sufficiently anaesthetised by alcohol, turn left out of the pub down the street to the stop where the bus turns round. Follow this street round to the right, between two rows of houses and leave Craster across the sports ground that slopes down to the sea. At Cullernose Point the path is hemmed in from the top of the low cliff by a fence, and after 300 yards it meets the road. It now lies parallel and close

CRASTER TO ALNMOUTH

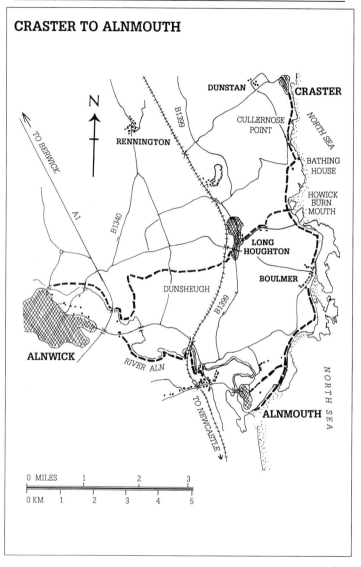

to the road, beneath some hawthorns, in early summer alive with stonechats, linnets and whitethroats. You turn away from the road to follow the coast as the road nears Howick and pass "The Bathing House", a wonderfully eroded house of sandstone at GR 263 175. Here a footpath sign directs you inland, along a track marked on the map as a black pecked line. At the end of the track you turn left and take the stony farm lane southwards as it descends gently towards the cove at the mouth of the Howick Burn and Sugar Sands. The track continues on the other side of a footbridge and takes you up a grassy slope to a path junction. Here you can divert from the final stage of the Reivers Way to walk inland into Alnwick, via Low Stead Farm and Longhoughton. Turn left in the village at the church and head straight ahead at the cross roads. Immediately after the cross roads is a path on the right to Dunsheugh and Snableazes and then on to a T-junction just before Denwick, where you turn left, then right at an electricity pylon to follow a fine path along the banks of the river beneath Alnwick Castle. This is open to the public every afternoon except Saturday. A riverside path returns you to Alnmouth from Alndyke (GR 208 126). This diversion adds almost ten miles to the day's distance.

However, from Sugar Sands the Reivers Way proper brings you through a parking area on the shore, and then between arable fields and the rocky shore into Boulmer. Ahead across the fields can be seen the gleaming yellow fuselages of the RAF air-sea rescue helicopters. Boulmer itself consists of The Fishing Boat Inn, a lifeboat shed across the road from the shore, a row of cottages and a small fleet of elegant cobles bobbing on the tide in Boulmer Haven. In the past the village was a haven for the smuggling of illicit liquor from the continent. Signs forbidding the digging of bait in the harbour glare at you, as though this is now the most heinous crime that could be committed in Boulmer. Heading south out of the village, turn left at a bus shelter and pass in front of a low cottage, and along the coast. When you reach Seaton Point, follow the farm track that leads inland, past Seaton House and rejoin the shore by the beach chalets. You reach a board warning of cliff erosion. From here you can follow the beach all the way to Alnmouth. As you approach the ancient Alnwick Golf Club at Foxton, you are walking along the top of the last beach on the Reivers Way. It is somehow fitting that the final stretch of this magnificent route through Northumberland is along a nondescript stretch of coast, with the fields of barley running flat to the sea. You could be in southern Sweden or Suffolk.

Alnmouth itself lies facing in towards the tiny estuary of the River Aln. Now the attention of the town has turned away from the river mouth which formerly provided its livelihood. You have the feeling that you do not want to linger: so many memories have been acquired on the way here, you want be away homewards rather than prolonging the finale. From the roundabout at the north end of the town, take the B1338 road over the tidal river Aln. Continue up to the roundabout at Hipsburn and walk straight ahead for 400 yards to reach the new station building down on the right. Thus the Reivers Way ends.

APPENDIX - ACCOMMODATION

The list below does not imply any recommendation by the author, unless mentioned in the text. Establishments are listed according to the order passed, starting the Reivers Way at Corbridge. Accommodation can often be found between the night halts implied in the text. These are listed under the settlement where the day starts. I doubt any two walkers will walk the Reivers Way in exactly the same stages. No attempt has been made to quote prices: in general, the more expensive establishments are listed first, which means hotels, followed by bed and breakfast establishments. There are campsites at Plankey Mill, Bardon Mill, Twice Brewed, Dunns Farm by Elsdon, Whitton by Rothbury, Clennel Hall, Alwinton, Wooler (Burnhouse Road), Belford, Waren Mill and Beadnell. In some of the wilder stretches of the walk it is certainly possible for the self-contained backpacker to camp wild, so long as he or she is discreet and leaves no evidence of ever having been there. All addresses below should have "Northumberland" added before the post code if writing to confirm accommodation.

CORBRIDGE

The Lion of Corbridge, Bridge End, Corbridge NE45 5LE - 0434 632 942

Riverside Hotel, Main Street, Corbridge NE45 5LE - 0434 632 942

The Angel Inn, Main Street Corbridge NE45 5LA - 0434 632 119

Wheatsheaf Hotel, St Helens Street, Corbridge NE45 5HE - 0434 632020

The Dyvels (GR 989 636), Station Road, Corbridge NE45 5AU -
0434 633 566

Pele Cottage (Mrs Anne Burton), Main Street, Corbridge NE45 5LA -
0434 633583

Holmlea (Mrs H.Stoker) Station Road, Corbridge NE45 5AY -
0434 632 486

Mrs J.Hunter, 1 Greencroft Avenue, Corbridge NE45 5DW -
0434 632 250

D.R.Maskell, 6 Greencroft Avenue, Corbridge NE45 5EW - 0434 632 205

Fellcroft (Mrs K.S.Wood), Station Road, Corbridge NE45 5AY -
0434 632 284

Dilston View (Mrs Ann Nixon) Station Road, Corbridge NE45 5AX -
0434 632 796

Gairshield (GR 92 57, Mrs Kristensen), Whitley Chapel NE47 0HS -
0434 673 562

Lord Crewe Arms (GR 96 50), Blanchland, County Durham DH8 9SP -
0434 683 392

ALLENDALE

Heatherlea Hotel (Mr and Mrs Butcher), Allendale NE47 9BJ -
0434 683 236

Bishopfield Country House Hotel (GR 826 526), Allendale NE47 9EJ -
0434 683 248

The King's Head Hotel, Market Place, Allendale NE47 9BD -
0434 683 681 Fax 685 314

Dale Hotel, Allendale - 0434 683212

Hotspur Hotel, Allendale - 0434 683355

Hare and Hounds, Allendale - 0434 683300

Crowberry Hall, Allendale, NE47 9SR - 0434 685200

Thornley House (Miss Eileen Flynn), Allendale NE47 9HN -
0434 683 255

The Old Hostel (GR 82 57, Mrs Dobbing), Catton NE47 9QQ -
0434 683 780

BARDON MILL

The Twice Brewed Hotel, Bardon Mill (GR 751 669) NE47 7AN -
0434 344534

Vallum Lodge Hotel, Twice Brewed, Bardon Mill (GR 747 668)
NE47 7AN - 0434 344248

Bowes Hotel (Mrs Miller), Bardon Mill NE47 7HU - 0434 344237

Beggar Bog Farm (GR 797 685, Mrs Huddleston), Bardon Mill
NE47 7NN - 0434 344320

Crindledykes (GR 782 682, Judy Davidson), Bardon Mill NE47 -
0434 344316

Winshields Farm (GR 744 669, Iona Lawson), Bardon Mill NE47 7AN -
0434 344243

Winshields Campsite, details as above.

Once Brewed Youth Hostel, Bardon Mill NE47 7AN - 0434 344360

Sewingshields Farm (GR 810 703, Mrs Lyn Murray) NE47 6NW -
0434 684418

Eldochan Hall (Mrs E.MacDonald) Willimontswick NE47 7DB -
0434 344465

WARK

The Battlesteads Hotel, Wark NE48 3LS - 0434 230209
The Knowesgate Hotel, Kirkwhelpington NE19 2SH (GR 988 857) -
0830 40261
Fox and Hounds Hotel, West Woodburn NE48 2RA (GR 89 86) -
0434 270210
The Bay Horse, West Woodburn NE48 2RX (GR 89 86) - 0434 270 218
Bellingham Youth Hostel (GR 844 835), Woodburn Road, Bellingham
NE48 2ED - 0434 220313

ELSDON

The Bird in Bush (public house), Elsdon NE19 - 0830 20478
Dunns Farm, Elsdon (GR 937 970) NE19 1AL - 0669 40219
Dunns Farm campsite, details as above.

ROTHBURY

The Railway Hotel, Bridge Street, Rothbury NE65 7LW - 0669 40264
Coquetvale Hotel, Station Road, Rothbury NE65 7QZ - 0669 20305
Orchard Guest House, High Street, Rothbury NE65 7RL - 0669 20684
The Haven, Backcroft, Rothbury NE65 7YA - 0669 20577
Whitton Farmhouse Hotel, Whitton, Rothbury (GR 057 012) -
0669 NE65 7RL
Tosson Tower Farm, Tosson (GR 055 011) Rothbury NE65 7NW -
0669 20228
Thropton Demesne (GR 025 024, Mr T Giles), Thropton - 0669 20196
Bickerton Cottage Farm, Thropton NE65 7LW - 0669 40264
Bounty Cottage (GR 95 03), Sharperton (Mrs Bradshaw) NE65 7AE -
0669 50388
Waterloo House (GR 93 04), Harbottle NE65 7DG - 0669 50322
Clennel Hall Campsite (Mrs Appleyard), Alwinton NE65 7BG -
0669 50341

USWAYFORD

Uswayford Farm (Mrs Buglass, GR 886 145) Harbottle NE65 7BU -
0669 50237

WOOLER

Tankerville Arms Hotel, 22 Cottage Road, Wooler NE71 6AD -
0668 81581

The Ryecroft Hotel, Ryecroft Way, Wooler NE71 6AB -
0668 81459/81233

The Red Lion Hotel, 1 High Street, Wooler NE71 6LD - 0668 81629

Loreto Guest House, 1 Ryecroft Way, Wooler - 0668 81350

Earle Hill Farm (GR 98 26, Mrs Armstrong,) Earle, Wooler - 0668 81243

Skirl Naked (Mrs Little, GR 980 253) Wooler NE71 6RE - 0668 81384

The Blue Bell Hotel, Belford - 0668 213543

The Black Swan Hotel, Market Place, Belford NE70 7ND - 0668 213 266

Detchant Farm (Mrs Jackson, GR 08 36) Belford NE70 7PF - 0668 213 261

Mrs B.Severs, 1 Church Street, Belford NE70 7LS - 0668 213013

Blue Bell Farmhouse, West Street, Belford NE70 7QE - 0668 213890

Mrs B.Ward, 20 Bell Road ,Belford NE70 7NY - 0668 21346

Easington Farm (GR 12 34, yes really! Mrs Oates,), Belford NE70 7EG -
0668 213 298

Mrs K.Godtschalk 5 Cragside Avenue, Belford NE70 7NA -
0668 213762

Mrs R.Shanks, 11 West Street, Belford NE70 7QA - 0668 213480

Mrs M.Tait, 24 West Street, Belford NE70 7QE - 0668 213397

Waren House Hotel, Waren Mill NE70 7EE - 0668 4581, Fax 4484

Mrs Knight, Rose Cottage, Waren Mill NE70 7EE - 0668 4473

Waren Caravan and Camping Park, Waren Mill - 06684 336,
Fax 06684 224

BAMBURGH

The Victoria Hotel, Bamburgh NE69 7BP - 0668 4431

The Lord Crewe Arms Hotel, Bamburgh - 0668 4393

The Mizen Head Hotel, Bamburgh - 0668 4254

Burton Hall, (GR178 331, Mrs Humphreys) Bamburgh NE69 7AR -
0668 4213

Glenander Guest House, 27 Lucker Road, Bamburgh NE69 7BS -
0668 4336

Mrs E.Walton, 34 Front Street, Bamburgh NE69 7BJ - 0668 4535

Mrs J.Hogg, The Hollies, 1 Ingram Road, Bamburgh NE69 7BU - 0668 4234

Mrs M.Tait, 1 Red Barns Crescent, Bamburgh NE69 7AY - 0668 4455

Mrs P.Armstrong, Sandford House, 20 Links Road Bamburgh NE69 7AX - 0668 4531

The St Aidan Hotel, Seahouses NE68 7SR - 0665 720355

The Olde Ship Hotel, Seahouses NE68 7RD - 0665 720200, Fax 721383

Links Hotel, 8 King St, Seahouses NE68 7XP - 0665 720530

Beach House Hotel, Seahouses - 0665 720337, Fax 720921

White Swan Hotel, Seahouses, NE66 7UB - 0665 720211

Mrs Oxley,Longstone Guest House, Main Street, Seahouses NE68 7RF - 0665 720212

Mrs Wood, Leehome 93 Main Street, Seahouses NE68 7TS - 0665 720230

Mrs B.Hogg, 8 North Lane, Seahouses NE68 - 0665 720719

Mrs M.Gregory, Homestead, 112 Main Street, Seahouses NE68 7TR - 0665 720776

Mrs C.Shiel, 36 Crumstone, Seahouses NE68 7SG - 0665 720519/ 720316

Mrs S.Bolton, 132 Main Street, North Sunderland, Seahouses NE68 7TZ - 0665 720729

Mrs Reay, 20 King Street, Seahouses NE68 7XP - 0665 720296

Mrs G.Swan, 12 King Street, Seahouses NE68 7XP - 0665 720201

Mrs M.Beecroft, 1a Southfield Avenue, Seahouses NE68 7YT - 0665 720259

Mrs L.Purvis, 133 Main Street, North Sunderland, Seahouses NE68 7TS - 0665 720912

Mrs S.Campbell, 29 St Aidans, Seahouses NE68 7SS - 720396

Mrs Hodgson, 99 Main Street, Seahouses NE68 7TS - 0665 721309/ 721266

Mrs M.Nichol, 174 Main Street, Seahouses NE68 7UA - 0665 720320

Mrs A.Douglas, 143 Main Street, Seahouses NE68 7TT - 0665 720059

Mrs M.Mole, Westside Guest House, 9 King Street, Seahouses NE68 7XN - 0665 720508

Beadnell Towers Hotel, Beadnell NE67 5AY - 0665 721211

Mrs R.Shell, Shepherd's Cottage, Beadnell NE67 5AD - 0665 720497

Mrs C.Field Beach Court, Harbour Road, Beadnell NE67 5BJ - 0665 720225

Mrs K.Thompson, Low Dover, Harbour Road, Beadnell NE67 5BH - 0665 720291

The Cottage Inn, Dunstan (by Craster, GR 247 197) - 066 576 203

ALNMOUTH

The Schooner Hotel, Northumberland St, NE66 2RS - 0665 830216

The Saddle Hotel, 24 Northumberland St, NE66 2RA - 0665 830 476

The Grange, Northumberland St, NE66 2RJ - 0665 830 401

Glendower Guest House, Argyle St, NE66 2SB - 0665 830 262

Blue Dolphins, 11 Riverside Road NE66 2SD - 0665 830 893

BIBLIOGRAPHY

You will be lucky indeed to find a copy of the original guide. *The Reivers Way* by H.O.Wade was published in 1977 by Frank Graham, 6 Queen's Terrace, Newcastle upon Tyne NE2 2PL, author. So far as I am aware, it was never reprinted.

Northumberland, The Buildings of England Series, Nikolaus Pevsner with Ian Richmond (Penguin 1957). More than worth the hunt through libraries and second hand shops - a superb guide which deserves to be republished.

A Portrait of Northumberland, Nancy Ridley (Robert Hale 3rd edn 1970) Valuable for its wealth of history of the 1715 and 1745 rebellions and history since that period.

The Borders, F.R.Banks (Batsford 1977). A valuable guide, packed with background information on the region.

Hadrian's Wall, James Forde Johnston, Book Club Associates, 1977. A copiously illustrated explanation of the wall.

Hadrian's Wall, David Breeze and Brian Dobson (Allen Lane, 1976) A scholarly and profound study of the wall

A Walk along the Wall, Hunter Davies (Batsford 1974 revised 1984) A personal, and highly enjoyable account of walking the wall in 1973 - now possibly more valuable as a portrait of the region twenty years ago than a discourse on the wall.

Along Hadrian's Wall, David Harrison (Cassell)

The Steel Bonnets, George Macdonald Fraser (Collins, 1989). A readable and informative discourse on the Border Reivers from the author of the excellent Flashman Papers.

LIST OF USEFUL ORDNANCE SURVEY MAPS

The Reivers Way represents remarkably good value in mapping - 150 miles in just four sheets. 1:25,000 are not available for all the route, and besides are not suitable. What is needed is the 1:50,000 Landranger series, sheet numbers 75 Berwick, 80 Cheviot and Kielder, 81 Alnwick and Rothbury, 87 Hexham and Haltwhistle. If you insisit on climbing the Cheviot as part of the Reivers Way you will need sheet 74 as well. I have found these maps en route in Corbridge, Allendale, Rothbury and Wooler. The maps accompanying the text should on no account be used for navigation. The way to walk this route is to buy all the OS maps before you depart, then, using the sketch maps and text and a highlighter pen, mark in the route.

CICERONE GUIDES

Cicerone publish a wide range of reliable guides to walking and climbing in Britain, and other general interest books.

LAKE DISTRICT - General Books
A DREAM OF EDEN
LAKELAND VILLAGES
LAKELAND TOWNS
REFLECTIONS ON THE LAKES
OUR CUMBRIA
THE HIGH FELLS OF LAKELAND
CONISTON COPPER A History
LAKELAND - A taste to remember (Recipes)
THE LOST RESORT?
CHRONICLES OF MILNTHORPE
LOST LANCASHIRE
THE PRIORY OF CARTMEL

LAKE DISTRICT - Guide Books
CASTLES IN CUMBRIA
THE CUMBRIA CYCLE WAY
WESTMORLAND HERITAGE WALK
IN SEARCH OF WESTMORLAND
CONISTON COPPER MINES Field Guide
SCRAMBLES IN THE LAKE DISTRICT
MORE SCRAMBLES IN THE LAKE DISTRICT
WINTER CLIMBS IN THE LAKE DISTRICT
WALKS IN SILVERDALE/ARNSIDE
BIRDS OF MORECAMBE BAY
THE EDEN WAY
WALKING ROUND THE LAKES

NORTHERN ENGLAND (outside the Lakes
BIRDWATCHING ON MERSEYSIDE
CANOEISTS GUIDE TO THE NORTH EAST
THE CLEVELAND WAY & MISSING LINK
THE DALES WAY
DOUGLAS VALLEY WAY
HADRIANS WALL Vol 1 The Wall Walk
HERITAGE TRAILS IN NW ENGLAND
THE ISLE OF MAN COASTAL PATH
THE LANCASTER CANAL
LAUGHS ALONG THE PENNINE WAY
A NORTHERN COAST-TO-COAST
NORTH YORK MOORS Walks
THE REIVERS WAY (Northumberland)
THE RIBBLE WAY
ROCK CLIMBS LANCASHIRE & NW
THE YORKSHIRE DALES A walker's guide
WALKING IN THE SOUTH PENNINES
WALKING IN THE NORTH PENNINES
WALKS IN THE YORKSHIRE DALES (3 VOL)
WALKS IN LANCASHIRE WITCH COUNTRY
WALKS TO YORKSHIRE WATERFALLS (2 vol)
WALKS ON THE WEST PENNINE MOORS
WALKING NORTHERN RAILWAYS EAST
WALKING NORTHERN RAILWAYS WEST

DERBYSHIRE & EAST MIDLANDS
WHITE PEAK WALKS - 2 Vols
HIGH PEAK WALKS
WHITE PEAK WAY
KINDER LOG

THE VIKING WAY
THE DEVIL'S MILL (Novel)
WHISTLING CLOUGH (Novel)
WALES & WEST MIDLANDS
THE RIDGES OF SNOWDONIA
HILLWALKING IN SNOWDONIA
HILL WALKING IN WALES (2 Vols)
ASCENT OF SNOWDON
WELSH WINTER CLIMBS
SNOWDONIA WHITE WATER SEA & SURF
SCRAMBLES IN SNOWDONIA
SARN HELEN Walking Roman Road
ROCK CLIMBS IN WEST MIDLANDS
THE SHROPSHIRE HILLS A Walker's Guide
HEREFORD & THE WYE VALLEY A Walker's Guide
THE WYE VALLEY WALK

SOUTH & SOUTH WEST ENGLAND
COTSWOLD WAY
EXMOOR & THE QUANTOCKS
THE KENNET & AVON WALK
THE SOUTHERN-COAST-TO-COAST
SOUTH DOWNS WAY & DOWNS LINK
SOUTH WEST WAY - 2 Vol
WALKING IN THE CHILTERNS
WALKING ON DARTMOOR
WALKERS GUIDE TO DARTMOOR PUBS
WALKS IN KENT
THE WEALDWAY & VANGUARD WAY

SCOTLAND
THE BORDER COUNTRY - WALKERS GUIDE
SCRAMBLES IN LOCHABER
SCRAMBLES IN SKYE
THE ISLAND OF RHUM
CAIRNGORMS WINTER CLIMBS
THE CAIRNGORM GLENS (Mountainbike Guide)
THE ATHOLL GLENS (Mountainbike Guide)
WINTER CLIMBS BEN NEVIS & GLENCOE
SCOTTISH RAILWAY WALKS
TORRIDON A Walker's Guide
SKI TOURING IN SCOTLAND

REGIONAL BOOKS UK & IRELAND
THE MOUNTAINS OF ENGLAND & WALES
VOL 1 WALES
VOL 2 ENGLAND
THE MOUNTAINS OF IRELAND
THE ALTERNATIVE PENNINE WAY
THE RELATIVE HILLS OF BRITAIN
LIMESTONE - 100 BEST CLIMBS

Also a full range of EUROPEAN and OVER-SEAS guidebooks - walking, long distance trails, scrambling, ice-climbing, rock climbing.

Other guides are constantly being added to the Cicerone List.
Available from bookshops, outdoor equipment shops or direct (send s.a.e. for price list) from
CICERONE, 2 POLICE SQUARE, MILNTHORPE, CUMBRIA, LA7 7PY

CICERONE GUIDES

Cicerone publish a wide range of reliable guides to walking and climbing abroad

FRANCE
TOUR OF MONT BLANC
CHAMONIX MONT BLANC - A Walking Guide
TOUR OF THE OISANS: GR54
WALKING THE FRENCH ALPS: GR5
THE CORSICAN HIGH LEVEL ROUTE: GR20
THE WAY OF ST JAMES: GR65
THE PYRENEAN TRAIL: GR10
THE RLS (Stevenson) TRAIL
TOUR OF THE QUEYRAS
ROCK CLIMBS IN THE VERDON
WALKS IN VOLCANO COUNTRY (Auvergne)
WALKING THE FRENCH GORGES (Provence)
FRENCH ROCK

FRANCE / SPAIN
WALKS AND CLIMBS IN THE PYRENEES
ROCK CLIMBS IN THE PYRENEES

SPAIN
WALKS & CLIMBS IN THE PICOS DE EUROPA
WALKING IN MALLORCA
BIRDWATCHING IN MALLORCA
COSTA BLANCA CLIMBS
ANDALUSIAN ROCK CLIMBS

FRANCE / SWITZERLAND
THE JURA - Walking the High Route and
 Winter Ski Traverses
CHAMONIX TO ZERMATT The Walker's Haute
Route

SWITZERLAND
WALKING IN THE BERNESE ALPS
CENTRAL SWITZERLAND
WALKS IN THE ENGADINE
WALKING IN TICINO
THE VALAIS - A Walking Guide
THE ALPINE PASS ROUTE

GERMANY / AUSTRIA
THE KALKALPEN TRAVERSE
KLETTERSTEIG - Scrambles
WALKING IN THE BLACK FOREST
MOUNTAIN WALKING IN AUSTRIA
WALKING IN THE SALZKAMMERGUT
KING LUDWIG WAY
HUT-TO-HUT IN THE STUBAI ALPS

ITALY & SLOVENIA
ALTA VIA - High Level Walkis in the Dolomites
VIA FERRATA - Scrambles in the Dolomites
ITALIAN ROCK - Rock Climbs in Northern Italy
CLASSIC CLIMBS IN THE DOLOMITES
WALKING IN THE DOLOMITES
THE JULIAN ALPS

MEDITERRANEAN COUNTRIES
THE MOUNTAINS OF GREECE
CRETE: Off the beaten track
TREKS & CLIMBS JORDAN
THE ATLAS MOUNTAINS
WALKS & CLIMBS IN THE ALA DAG (Turkey)

OTHER COUNTRIES
ADVENTURE TREKS - W. N. AMERICA
ADVENTURE TREKS - NEPAL
ANNAPURNA TREKKERS GUIDE
CLASSIC TRAMPS IN NEW ZEALAND
TREKKING IN THE CAUCAUSUS

GENERAL OUTDOOR BOOKS
THE HILL WALKERS MANUAL
FIRST AID FOR HILLWALKERS
MOUNTAIN WEATHER
MOUNTAINEERING LITERATURE
THE ADVENTURE ALTERNATIVE
MODERN ALPINE CLIMBING
ROPE TECHNIQUES IN MOUNTAINEERING
MODERN SNOW & ICE TECHNIQUES
LIMESTONE -100 BEST CLIMBS IN BRITAIN

CANOEING
SNOWDONIA WILD WATER, SEA & SURF
WILDWATER CANOEING
CANOEIST'S GUIDE TO THE NORTH EAST

CARTOON BOOKS
ON FOOT & FINGER
ON MORE FEET & FINGERS
LAUGHS ALONG THE PENNINE WAY

---

*Also a full range of guidebooks
to walking, scrambling, ice-climbing,
rock climbing, and other adventurous
pursuits in Britain and abroad*

---

*Other guides are constantly being added to the Cicerone List.
Available from bookshops, outdoor equipment shops or direct (send for price list)
from CICERONE, 2 POLICE SQUARE, MILNTHORPE, CUMBRIA, LA7 7PY*

Printed by CARNMOR PRINT & DESIGN, 95-97 LONDON ROAD, PRESTON, LANCASHIRE, UK.